MW00399347

Talking About Buddhism—Q&A

装幀 ● 菊地信義
装画 ● 野村俊夫

翻訳 ● James M. Vardaman, Jr.
イラスト ● 青木宣人
　　　　　高橋　満

編集 ● 翻訳情報センター

Published by Kodansha International Ltd.,
17-14, Otowa 1-chome, Bunkyo-ku, Tokyo 112-8652.
No part of this publication may be reproduced
in any form or by any means without permission
in writing from the publisher.
Copyright © 1997 by Takada Yoshihito and James M. Vardaman, Jr.
All rights reserved. Printed in Japan.

First Edition 1997

ISBN4-7700-2161-5
99 00　10 9 8 7 6 5 4 3 2

英語で話す「仏教」Q&A
Talking About Buddhism — Q&A

高田佳人 [著]
ジェームス・M・バーダマン [訳]

Bilingual
Books

まえがき

　生まれた時にはお宮参りをし、結婚式は教会で挙げ、お葬式はお寺でするという日本人の生活は、外国人の目には不思議に映るようです。「どうしてそんなことが出来るの？」と外国人から質問され、はたと考え込んでしまう日本人も少なくありません。

　日本に伝来した仏教は、日本人に生きる知恵と力を与え続けました。仏教は日本人の心を癒し、またものの見方、考え方に多大の影響を与えてきました。日本を語るときに仏教は欠かせません。

　仏教の開祖は言うまでもなくインドの釈迦です。釈迦が悟りを開いたのは、キリストの誕生のさらに500年ほど前の、今からおよそ2500年前のことでした。その後、仏教は国境を越えてアジア全土に広まりました。教えのポイントこそ普遍的ですが、仏教は、それぞれの時代、それぞれの国の文明・文化と混交し、様々に形を変えながらそれぞれの地域の人々に受容されてきました。近年欧米でも、その仏教思想が見直されています。

　本書はこれだけは知っておきたい仏教に関することがらを、平易に整理して、やさしい英語で説明できるようにしてあります。

　海外に駐在したり、留学やホームステイをすると、宗教の話題が必ず出てきます。本書が国際交流に携わる人々やビジネスマンの異文化コミュニケーションに、また英語を学習中の人に、必携の書となるものと期待しています。

　なお、この本の内容につきましては、横山紘一先生のご校閲をいただきました。厚く御礼申し上げます。

　　　　　　　　　　　　　　　　　　　　　　高田　佳人

Preface

In the eyes of non-Japanese, it seems odd that when Japanese are born they are taken to a shrine, when they marry they go to a church, and when they die they go to a temple. When asked, "Why do you do that?" most Japanese are utterly at a loss as to how to answer.

The Buddhism that was transmitted to Japan has continued to provide Japanese with wisdom and strength for living. Buddhism has soothed the minds of the people and greatly affected their way of seeing and thinking. No discussion of Japan can overlook Buddhism.

Needless to say, the Buddha of India was the founder of the religion. He attained enlightenment some five hundred years before the birth of Christ and approximately 2,500 years before our time. Buddhism was to cross national borders and spread throughout Asia. Its teachings are universal, yet it has transformed itself through the generations and the civilizations and cultures of various countries, and has been accepted in different forms by the peoples of those lands. In recent years, even in the West, Buddhist thought has undergone a new appraisal.

The present volume includes the essential points that one should know about Buddhism so that one can explain them in straightforward, simple English.

Whether one is working, studying or living with a family abroad, the matter of religion will invariably arise. It is hoped that this book will be of value to those who are involved in international relations and businessmen who deal with people of other cultures, as well as those who are studying English.

I would like to express my deep gratitude to Professor Yokoyama Kōitsu for his comments and suggestions on this manuscript.

Takada Yoshihito

目　次

まえがき　　4

1．釈迦の一生

Q：釈迦はいつ、どこで生まれたのですか？　　18
Q：釈迦が生まれたのはどんな時代でしたか？　　20

Q：シッダールタは母親の右脇から生まれたそうですが、ほんとうですか？　　22
Q：シッダールタにはどんな家族がいたのですか？　　24
Q：シッダールタが出家したのはなぜですか？　　26
Q：シッダールタはどうやって悟りを開いたのですか？　　28
Q：悟りを開いたあと、シッダールタはどんな人生を送ったのですか？　　30
Q：釈迦の弟子になったのはどんな人たちですか？　　32

Q：釈迦はいくつまで生き、どのようにして亡くなったのですか？　　34
Q：釈迦が亡くなった時、どんな遺言を残したのでしょうか？　　36

2．仏教の基本的な教え

Q：仏教とは、一口に言ってどういうものなのですか？　　40
Q：なぜ釈迦を「仏」と呼ぶのですか？　　42
Q：釈迦以外にも仏と呼ばれる人はいるのですか？　　42

Contents

Preface   5

1. The Life of the Buddha

Q : When and where was the Buddha born?   19
Q : What were the times like when the Buddha was born?
21
Q : Is it true that the Buddha was born from his mother's right
side?   23
Q : What kind of family did Siddhartha have?   25
Q : Why did Siddhartha renounce the world?   27
Q : How did Siddhartha achieve enlightenment?   29
Q : What kind of life did Siddhartha lead after his awakening?
31
Q : What kinds of people became the Buddha's disciples?
33
Q : How long did the Buddha live and how did he die?   35

Q : What were the parting words of the Buddha?   37

2. The Essential Teachings of Buddhism

Q : In a nutshell, what is Buddhism?   41
Q : Why is the Buddha also called *hotoke*?   43
Q : Is there anyone other than the Buddha who is called a
buddha?   43

Q：阿弥陀仏と言ったり阿弥陀如来と言ったりしますが、「仏」
と「如来」とはどう違うのですか？　44

Q：「涅槃」とはどんなことですか？　46
Q：「解脱」とはどんなことですか？　48
Q：「悟り」とはどんなことですか？　50
Q：釈迦が悟ったこととはどんなことだったのですか？　52
Q：「四諦」とはどんなことですか？　54
Q：「八正道」とはどんなことですか？　54
Q：「十二因縁（十二縁起）」とはなんですか？　56
Q：十二因縁の12の段階とはどんなものなのでしょうか？
58
Q：「無常」とはどういうことですか？　60
Q：「無我」とはどういうことですか？　60
Q：仏教は「苦」を説くと聞きますが、なぜですか？　62
Q：「縁起」とは仏教の言葉なのですか？　64

Q：「因果応報」とはなんですか？　66
Q：仏教で菩提樹が大事にされるのはなぜですか？　66
Q：経典とはなんですか？　68

3．仏教の発展と日本への伝来

Q：インドに生まれた仏教は、どのように世界に伝わっていき
ましたか？　70
Q：大乗仏教と小乗仏教（上座部仏教）の違いを説明してくだ
さい。　72

Q：「菩薩」とはどんな人ですか？　74
Q：「南無阿弥陀仏」とか「南無妙法蓮華経」とかいいますが、
なんのことですか？　76
Q：大乗仏教の経典とはどんなものですか？　78

Q: People sometimes say Amida Buddha and Amida Tathagata, but what exactly is the difference between "buddha" and "tathagata"?   45

Q: What is "nirvana"?   47

Q: What is "emancipation"?   49

Q: What is "enlightenment"?   51

Q: What was it that the Buddha awakened to?   53

Q: What are the Four Noble Truths (*shitai*)?   55

Q: What is the Eightfold Nobel Path?   55

Q: What is the Law of the Twelve Causes?   57

Q: What are the twelve stages in the Law of the Twelve Causes?   59

Q: What is impermanence?   61

Q: What is "nothing has an ego"?   61

Q: Why is it that Buddhism preaches "suffering"?   63

Q: Does the word "origin" (*engi*) come from Buddhism?   65

Q: What is "karmic retribution"?   67

Q: Why is the bodhi tree made much of in Buddhism?   67

Q: What are sutras?   69

3. The Development of Buddhism and Its Introduction to Japan

Q: How was Buddhism, which was born in India, transmitted to the world?   71

Q: Could you please explain the difference between Mahayana Buddhism and Hinayana (Theravada) Buddhism ?   73

Q: What kind of person is a bodhisattva?   75

Q: Why do people say "*Namu Amida Butsu*" and "*Namu Myōhō Renge-kyō*"?   77

Q: What are Mahayana sutras like?   79

Q：仏教は、いつどこから日本に伝わってきたのですか？
　82
Q：なぜ日本は仏教を受け入れたのですか？　　84
Q：仏教はどのようにして日本に根づいていきましたか？
　86

4．日本の仏教を作った人たち

Q：空海はどんな人でしたか？　　102
Q：最澄はどんな人でしたか？　　104
Q：法然はどんな人でしたか？　　106
Q：親鸞はどんな人でしたか？　　110
Q：日蓮はどんな人でしたか？　　112
Q：一遍はどんな人でしたか？　　114
Q：栄西はどんな人でしたか？　　116
Q：道元はどんな人でしたか？　　118

5．仏教の宗派の特徴

Q：華厳宗とはどんな宗派ですか？　　122
Q：法相宗とはどんな宗派ですか？　　124
Q：律宗とはどんな宗派ですか？　　126
Q：真言宗とはどんな宗派ですか？　　128
Q：天台宗とはどんな宗派ですか？　　130
Q：浄土宗とはどんな宗派ですか？　　132
Q：浄土真宗とはどんな宗派ですか？　　134
Q：日蓮宗とはどんな宗派ですか？　　138
Q：時宗とはどんな宗派ですか？　　140
Q：臨済宗とはどんな宗派ですか？　　140
Q：曹洞宗とはどんな宗派ですか？　　142

Q: When and from where was Buddhism introduced into Japan?   83
Q: Why did Japan accept Buddhism?   85
Q: How did Buddhism establish roots in Japan?   87

4. The Makers of Japanese Buddhism

Q: What kind of person was Kūkai?   103
Q: What kind of person was Saichō?   105
Q: What kind of person was Hōnen?   107
Q: What kind of person was Shinran?   111
Q: What kind of person was Nichiren?   113
Q: What kind of person was Ippen?   115
Q: What kind of person was Eisai?   117
Q: What kind of person was Dōgen?   119

5. Features of the Sects of Buddhism

Q: What is the Kegon sect?   123
Q: What is the Hossō sect?   125
Q: What is the Ritsu sect?   127
Q: What is the Shingon sect?   129
Q: What is the Tendai sect?   131
Q: What is the Jōdo sect?   133
Q: What is the Jōdo Shin sect?   135
Q: What is the Nichiren sect?   139
Q: What is the Ji sect?   141
Q: What is the Rinzai sect?   141
Q: What is the Sōtō sect?   143

6. 寺と僧侶

Q：寺はどのようにして発生してきたのですか？　146

Q：寺にはよく五重の塔がありますが、なんのためにあるのですか？　148

Q：寺はどうやって収入を得ているのですか？　150

Q：僧とはいったいどんな存在ですか？　152

Q：僧になる（出家する）ことに、どういう意味があるのですか？　154

Q：戒律とはなんですか？　156

Q：僧が髪を剃るのはなぜですか？　158

Q：袈裟にはどういう意味があるのですか？　160

Q：数珠はなんのために持つのですか？　162

7. 仏教と庶民の生活・行事

Q：仏教では、人が死んだあとのことをどう考えていますか？　164

Q：地獄とはどんなところですか？　166

Q：極楽浄土とはどんなところですか？　168

Q：仏教ではどうしてお墓を作るのですか？　170

Q：葬式後、四十九日とか三回忌とか、何度も法事をするのはなぜですか？　172

Q：仏壇はいつごろから家に置かれるようになったのですか？　174

Q：位牌とはなんですか？　176

Q：戒名（法名・法号）とはなんですか？　176

Q：不祝儀袋の「御霊前」と「御仏前」はどう使い分ければいいのですか？　178

6. Temples and Priests

Q : Where did temples come from?   147

Q : Temples often have pagodas, but what are they for?
   149

Q : How do temples obtain income?   151

Q : What exactly is a priest?   153

Q : What does it mean to become a priest (renounce the world)?   155

Q : What are "precepts" (*kairitsu*)?   157

Q : Why do priests shave their heads?   159

Q : What is the symbolism of the Buddhist surplice (*kesa*)?
   161

Q : Why do they carry a string of beads?   163

7. Buddhism and the Life and Ceremonies of the People

Q : In Buddhism, what happens after a person dies?   165

Q : What kind of place is hell?   167

Q : What kind of place is the Pure Land?   169

Q : In Buddhism, why does one make a grave?   171

Q : Why are Buddhist services held so often, for example on the 49th day and the third anniversary after death?   173

Q : When did Buddhist altars come to be placed in homes?
   175

Q : What is a memorial tablet?   177

Q : What is the Buddhist name that is posthumously given?
   177

Q : What is the difference between *Goreizen* and *Gobutsuzen* on the *Bushūgi-bukuro*?   179

Q：霊のたたりは本当にあるのですか？　180

Q：水子地蔵とはなんですか？　182
Q：精進料理とはなんですか？　184
Q：死者はなぜ北枕で寝るのですか？　186

Q：坐禅はどうすればいいのですか？　186
Q：除夜の鐘は、なぜ108回ならすのですか？　188

Q：「お盆」の意味を教えてください。　190
Q：「お彼岸」の意味を教えてください。　190
Q：「花祭り」の意味を教えてください。　192

8. 仏教と神道、キリスト教

Q：仏教と神道の根本的な違いはどこにありますか？　196

Q：お経と祝詞はどう違いますか？　198
Q：僧侶と神主はどう違うのですか？　200

Q：合掌と柏手の違いはどんなところにありますか？　202

Q：神道には女神がいるのに、なぜ菩薩は男ばかりなのです
　か？　204
Q：仏教には仏像があるのに、神道には神像はないのですか？
　206
Q：仏壇と神棚が1つの家にあっても、日本ではなぜおかしく
　ないのですか？　208
Q：檀家と氏子とはどう違うのですか？　210
Q：仏教とキリスト教の根本的な違いは？　210

Q：釈迦とイエス・キリストの共通点と違いはどこにあります
　か？　212

Q: Is there really such a thing as being cursed by a spirit?
181

Q: What is a *Mizuko Jizō*?   183

Q: What is *shōjin ryōri*?   185

Q: Why are the dead placed with the pillow to the north?
187

Q: What is the proper way to do seated meditation?   187

Q: Why is the bell struck 108 times at "*joya no kane*"?
189

Q: What is the meaning of *O-bon*?   191

Q: What is the meaning of *O-higan*?   191

Q: Please explain the meaning of *Hana Matsuri*.   193

8. Buddhism, Shintō and Christianity

Q: What are the fundamental differences between Buddhism
and Shintoism?   197

Q: What is the difference between sutras and *norito*?   199

Q: What is the difference between Buddhist priests and
Shintō priests?   201

Q: What is the difference between *gasshō* and *kashiwade*?
203

Q: Why is it that there are female deities in Shintō, but
bodhisattvas are always male?   205

Q: Why are there images of the Buddha, but no images of the
gods?   207

Q: Why don't Japanese think it strange to have a Buddhist
altar and a Shintō altar in the same house?   209

Q: What is the difference between *danka* and *ujiko*?   211

Q: What is the fundamental difference between Buddhism
and Christianity?   211

Q: What are the similarities and dissimilarities between the
Buddha and Jesus Christ?   213

Q：聖書とお経はどう違いますか？　　214

Q：「愛」という言葉の意味は、キリスト教と仏教ではどう違
　いますか？　　216

Q：日本人は結婚式を神式でするのに、お葬式はなぜ仏式です
　るのですか？　　218

索引　　222

Q: What differences are there between the Bible and sutras? 215

Q: What is the difference between the word "love" in the Christian sense and in the Buddhist sense?   217

Q: Why is it that Japanese have Shintō weddings, and Buddhist funerals?   219

Index   222

釈迦の一生

The Life of the Buddha

Q: 釈迦はいつ、どこで生まれたのですか？

　　一説によると、釈迦は紀元前463年、インド
に生まれ、80歳で亡くなったとされています。
今から2400年ほど前、キリストよりも約400年
以前に活躍した人と考えればいいと思います。

　　現在のネパール領タラーイ地方とインド領の
接する辺りに、当時シャークヤ国という小部族
国家がありました。釈迦はこの国の指導者の息
子、つまり王子として生まれたのです。

　　この部族の名を中国人が漢字で「釈迦」と表
したことから、私たちが今使っている「釈迦」
という呼び方が生まれました。

Q: When and where was the Buddha born?

According to one tradition, the Buddha was born in India in 463 B.C. and died at the age of eighty. Whatever the details, it can be said that the Buddha was active some 2,400 years ago, approximately 400 years before Christ.

In the region where present-day Tarai in Nepal borders on India, there was at that time a state ruled by the Sakya Tribe. The Buddha was the son of the tribal chief and was therefore a prince.

The Chinese called this tribe *Shaka* in Chinese characters, and that custom has been followed by the Japanese people.

　父はシュッドーダナ王、母はマーヤー夫人といい、彼はその一粒種でした。シッダールタと名づけられ、父の氏姓がガウタマでしたので、彼はガウタマ・シッダールタと呼ばれました。

　お城があった場所はカピラヴァスツといい、この城は日本では通称カピラ城と呼ばれています。シャークヤ国（釈迦国）は小さな国ですが、共和制を敷いており、部族内の有力者が公会堂に集まって話し合いで政治を行っていたと言われています。ですから、いわゆる専制君主国の絶対的権力を持った王や王子というイメージとは、かなり異なるようです。

Q: 釈迦が生まれたのはどんな時代でしたか？

　この時代は農業生産が拡大し、手工業も飛躍的に発展しました。やがて、生産された製品を売買する商人が登場します。商人たちはキャラバンを組織し、町や村を行き来して盛んに交易を行いました。彼らは交易の安全を図るために王族と結びついて保護を得、王族たちは財政的な恩恵に浴したのです。そうして力を持った大きな部族は、小さな部族を併合し、次第に国家が成立していきます。

　当時、この地域を支配していたのは、インド・ヨーロッパ語族の言語を話す先史時代の民族アーリア人です。彼らは紀元前15世紀ころからインドに進入し、自分たちを頂点とする身分階級制度を作りました。

　カーストと呼ばれるこの制度は、バラモン（司祭）、クシャトリア（王侯）、ヴァイシャ（庶民）、シュードラ（隷民）に代表され、釈迦はクシャトリアだったといわれています。

He was the only son of King Suddhodana and Queen Maya. Since he was named Siddhartha and his father's surname was Gautama, he was called Gautama Siddhartha.

The palace was located in Kapilavastu, known in Japan as Kapila Palace. The country of the Sakyas was a small kingdom, but it had a republican form of government in which tribal leaders gathered in an assembly hall to discuss government policy. It was considerably different from the common image of kings and princes wielding absolute power under a monarchy.

Q: What were the times like when the Buddha was born?

It was a period when agricultural production was expanding and handicraft skills were advancing rapidly. In due course, there appeared merchants who bought and sold the goods that were produced. These merchants organized caravans which traveled between towns and villages carrying on a brisk trade. In order to carry out this trade in safety, the merchants developed ties with the king and received royal protection and in return the royal family enjoyed economic benefits. The larger tribe that came to power in this way then began to merge with smaller tribes, gradually forming a large state.

An Indo-European speaking Aryan people occupied this area in pre-history. Commencing in about the 15th century B.C., they invaded India and created a class society with themselves at the top.

This "caste" system, as it is called, consisted of the Brahman (priests), Kshatriya (royalty), Vaisya (commoners) and Sudra (the lower class), and it is said that the Sakyas were Kshatriya.

アーリア人はインドにヒンドゥー教をもたらしました。この宗教は多神教の民族宗教で、今でもインド人の80パーセント以上がヒンドゥー教徒だとされています。当時はバラモンの儀式が人々の生活を律していたため、このころのヒンドゥー教をバラモン教とも呼んでいます。このように、当時は政治、経済、宗教、文化と、あらゆる面で発展・高揚の途上にあった時代だったといえます。

また、当時アーリア人は、人々の祈願を聞き届けるための祭式や、神々への讃歌や典礼を示した聖典など、いわゆるヒンドゥー教とそれにまつわる文化を、古代の文章語であるサンスクリット語で伝えていました。サンスクリット語は聖なる言葉とされ、仏教の聖典もこの言葉で伝えられています。

しかし、後にはより大衆的な言葉であるパーリ語によって伝道されるようになり、一部の仏教思想はパーリ語によってスリランカを通じて東南アジア各地に広められています。ですから、仏教にはサンスクリット語による文献とパーリ語による文献、それに中国に渡って中国語で伝えられたものとさまざまなものがあるのです。

Q: シッダールタは母親の右脇から生まれたそうですが、ほんとうですか？

カピラ城から東に20キロほど行ったところに、ルンビニーという林苑があります。ここが釈迦の生まれたところで、現在も参拝地として人が訪れますが、閑散とした草原と化しているといったほうがよいような状態です。

シッダールタの母であるマーヤー夫人は、シ

The Aryans brought Hindu beliefs into India. Hinduism is a polytheistic folk religion and even today over 80% of the people of India are believers. At the time, the daily lives of the people were carried out in accordance with Brahman rites, so the Hinduism of this period is referred to as Brahmanism. Hence, it can be said that this period was one of development and enhancement in government, economics, religion, culture and every other aspect.

The Aryans of that day transmitted via Sanskrit, an ancient written language, the rites that were carried out to convey the entreaties of the people and the scriptures which exhibited the poems of praise and proper movements for approaching the gods, that is, the Hindu religion and the culture revolving around it. Sanskrit was considered a sacred language, and Buddhist scriptures came to be transmitted in it as well.

However, at a later time teachings were transmitted in Pali, a language of the masses, and it was in Pali that portions of Buddhist thought were transmitted to Sri Lanka and to other parts of Southeast Asia. Buddhism was therefore transmitted in three ways: through the languages of Sanskrit, Pali and Chinese.

Q: Is it true that the Buddha was born from his mother's right side?

Approximately twenty kilometers east of Kapila Palace at Kapilavastu is the forested garden park called Lumbini. This is where the Buddha was born and where people still come to worship, but it has now been transformed into a quiet, grassy plain.

Siddhartha's mother, Queen Maya, was a princess of the

ャークヤ国の東隣のコーリヤ族の出身で、出産
のために里帰りをしようとして侍女たちを連れ
て途中このルンビニー苑へ立ち寄ったのだそう
です。

　当時そこは花の咲き乱れる林苑で、かぐわし
い香りが辺り一面に漂っていました。マーヤー
夫人がふと1本の木に右手を差しかけた時、そ
の右脇が七色に輝き出し、やがてその光の中か
ら玉のような男の子が姿を現しました。それが
シッダールタで、後の釈迦であったと言われて
いるのです。

　その子はすぐに立ち上がり、右手で天を指
し、左手で地を指して7歩あゆみ、「天上天下
唯我独尊」と言ったと伝えられていますが、い
ずれも後世、釈迦を神格化して作られた伝承だ
と思われます。イエス・キリストも処女である
マリアから生まれたといわれますが、両者とも
私たちのような凡人とは異なった生まれ方をし
た、聖なる存在であることを強調した伝説なの
でしょう。

Q: シッダールタにはどんな家族がいたのですか？

　父シュッドーダナ王、母マーヤー夫人がシッ
ダールタにとっての最初の家族だったのです
が、マーヤー夫人はシッダールタを生んで間も
なく亡くなってしまいます。

　その後、シュッドーダナ王はマーヤー夫人の
妹のマハー・プラジャーパティーを後妻としま
した。幼いシッダールタは、叔母であるマハ
ー・プラジャーパティーに養育されることにな
ったわけです。

　シュッドーダナ王とマハー・プラジャーパテ
ィーの間にも子供が生まれました。シッダール

kingdom of Koliya to the east. It is said that she, together with her attendants, stopped to rest in the Lumbini Garden on the way to Koliya where she intended to give birth.

In those days the garden was resplendent with flowers and the entire area was filled with fragrance. When Queen Maya suddenly put out her right hand and touched a tree, her side emitted a seven-colored light and from that light there appeared the figure of a jewel-like boy. This child was Siddhartha, later to become the Buddha.

It is also said that the child immediately stood up, and with his right hand raised toward heaven and his left pointing toward earth, he took seven steps and declared, "In heaven and on earth, I alone am honored." These stories may be considered traditions created and handed down to glorify the Buddha after his life on earth. Just as it is said that Jesus Christ was born of the Virgin Mary, the legend stresses that he is a sacred being born in a different way from ordinary beings.

Q: What kind of family did Siddhartha have?

Siddhartha's own family consisted of King Suddhodana and Queen Maya, but soon after giving birth to Siddhartha, Queen Maya died.

King Suddhodana later took Queen Maya's sister Mahaprajapati as his second wife, and so it was that the infant Siddhartha came to be raised by his foster mother Mahaprajapati.

A child was also born to King Suddhodana and Mahaprajapati, and this was his half-brother. The king's love for his

タに腹違いの弟ができたわけです。しかし、父
王のシッダールタに対する愛情は特別で、彼に
は雨期を過ごすための館、乾期を過ごすための
館、冬期を過ごすための館という3つの館が与
えられていたといいます。

　青年期に達したシッダールタは、人生上の問
題を真剣に考え、思い悩む性格だったようで
す。それを心配した父王は、シッダールタに結
婚を勧めました。シッダールタも承諾して、ヤ
ショーダラーという名の美しい妃をめとりまし
た。やがて2人の間には、ラーフラと名づけら
れた息子が生まれます。カピラ城に住むこれら
の人々が、シッダールタの家族だったわけで
す。

Q: シッダールタが出家したのはなぜですか？

　カピラ城で親子3世代の家族が幸せに暮らし
ていたのですが、シッダールタはそのような世
間的な幸せには満足できませんでした。人間は
なぜ苦悩を背負って生きなければならないのか
と思い悩み、その悩みや苦しみを解決する道を
模索するようになっていたのです。

　ある日、彼は東の門から城を出ました。その
時、彼は、老いさらばえた体を杖でやっと支え
て歩く老人を目にしました。彼はだれしもがこ
のように老いなければならない運命を思い、暗
い思いに沈みました。

　またある日、南の門から城を出ると、今度は
苦痛にもだえる病人と出会いました。そしてや
はり、万人がいつかは病苦と闘わなければなら
ないことを思って心を痛めました。

　次にシッダールタが西の門から城を出た時、
人々が泣いて死者にとりすがっていました。彼

first son, however, was special, and it is said he provided Siddhartha with three palaces——one each for the rainy season, the dry season, and the winter.

When he became a young man, Siddhartha began to exhibit unusual sensitivity and contemplative concern for the problems of human existence. Out of concern, his father encouraged him to marry. Siddhartha complied and took as his wife a beautiful princess named Yasodhara. Presently a son named Rahula was born to them. These were the members of the family that lived in Kapila Palace.

Q: Why did Siddhartha renounce the world?

This three-generation family lived together happily in Kapila Palace, but Siddhartha was not satisfied with such worldly happiness. He agonized over why it was that human beings had to bear suffering throughout life and began groping for a way to ease this suffering and hardship.

One day when the prince left the eastern gate of the palace, he saw a thin, decrepit old man barely able to totter along with a cane. Realizing that it was everyone's destiny to grow old like that, Siddhartha fell into dark contemplation.

Another day, upon leaving the southern gate of the palace, he encountered a sick person in great suffering. It pained him once more to realize that at some time everyone has to struggle with the pains of illness.

On the next occasion, when he departed through the western gate, he encountered people crying during a funeral pro-

はこの時も、あらゆる人が死を避けることができないことを知って唇をかんだのです。彼は城の門外に、老・病・死という人間の根源的な苦を見たのです。

　最後に北の門から城を出た時、彼は今度は1人の修行者を目にしました。その修行者は堂々として美しく、一点の迷いも見あたりません。それを見た時、彼は、世間を離れて修行を積み、真理を求めることの中にしか苦を離れる道がないことを直観しました。そしてある夜、彼は愛馬にまたがり、御者を連れて家を出たのです。シッダールタが29歳の時でした。

Q: シッダールタはどうやって悟(さと)りを開いたのですか？

　シッダールタは熾烈(しれつ)な苦行(くぎょう)を行いました。苦行の中心は断食(だんじき)で、1日に穀類1粒だけを食べて瞑想にふけっていたという言い伝えもあります。パキスタン北西部のペシャワール地方にあったガンダーラからは、骨と皮ばかりになった彼の坐禅像が出土しています。

　シッダールタには5人の修行仲間がいたのですが、彼らは何度も苦行で瀕死(ひんし)の状態に陥ったシッダールタを見て、彼が死んでしまったと思ったといいます。

　彼の苦行は6年間に及びました。しかし、彼はやがて苦行によっては悟りを得ることができないと実感し、苦行を捨てることにしました。

　彼は山を下り、近くを流れるナイランジャナー河で身を清め、苦行で弱った体を休めていました。するとそこにスジャーターという名の娘が通りかかり、彼に乳がゆを供養してくれました。彼はこれを食べて元気を取り戻したので

cession. He bit his lip when he realized that no human being is able to escape from death. Outside the palace gates Siddhartha witnessed the fundamental human sufferings of aging, illness and death.

Finally, when he went out the northern palace gate, Siddhartha saw an ascetic. This monk seemed majestic and splendid and possessed of not a single illusion. At that moment, he realized intuitively that the only way to escape from suffering was to withdraw from the world, accumulate ascetic practices and search for truth. And so one night he mounted his favorite horse and accompanied by his personal servant, he left the palace. Gautama Siddhartha was twenty-nine at that time.

Q: How did Siddhartha achieve enlightenment?

Siddhartha underwent severe austerities. Chief among these was fasting, and one legend has it that he ate only one grain of rice a day and immersed himself in meditation. A statue of the Buddha unearthed in Gandhara in the Peshawar region of northwest Pakistan shows him wasted to skin and bones in seated meditation.

Siddhartha had five ascetic companions and it is said that upon seeing his condition following his repeated austerities they thought he had died.

He continued his austere practices for six years. However, he ultimately realized that one cannot attain enlightenment through self-mortification and he determined to give up his ascetic practices.

Coming down from the mountains, he cleaned himself in the nearby Nairanjana River and was resting his body weakened from austerities. A young woman named Sujata happened by and made him an offering of rice boiled in milk. Eating this, he was mentally and physically refreshed.

す。

　それから彼は1本の菩提樹に歩み寄り、その下で坐禅を組みました。そして瞑想に入り、人間の真実、宇宙の真理に思いをこらしたのです。

　経典によると、悪魔が瞑想中のシッダールタを襲い、あるいは誘惑して悟りを妨害しようとしたそうですが、これは恐らく彼自身が心の中で、自分の逃避心や欲望などの煩悩と戦った葛藤を表現したものではないでしょうか。

　こうして菩提樹の下に座って7日目、明けの明星が輝くころ、シッダールタはついに万物についての真理を悟ったのです。時に35歳でした。わが国では、彼が悟りを開いたこの日を12月8日と特定して、「成道会」と呼んでお祝いしています。

Q: 悟りを開いたあと、シッダールタはどんな人生を送ったのですか?

　悟りを開いたあと、シッダールタは自分の悟りの内容があまりにも深遠なので、人々に話しても理解してもらうことができないと考えました。だから、彼はそのことを自分1人の胸に秘めておこうと密かに決めたのです。

　ところが、これを察した梵天(神々の最高位にあるとされる神)がシッダールタの前に姿を現し、彼が悟った内容を人々に説き、苦しみにあえぐ人々を救済するように訴えました。

　彼はこの梵天の言葉に従い、自分の悟った内容を人々に説き示し、自分と同じ境地に彼らを導くことを決意したのです。つまり、生きとし生けるものを悟りに導くために、伝道をすることを決意したのです。

He then came upon a bodhi (*bo*) tree under which he sat and began to meditate. Entering into meditation, he concentrated his mind on the truths of human beings and the universe.

According to the scriptures, as he was meditating evil spirits attacked him and tempted him in an attempt to hinder his enlightenment. Perhaps this should be taken as representing the struggle within himself to overcome such delusions as evasiveness and desire.

And so it happened that on the seventh day of seated contemplation, just as the morning star appeared at daybreak, Siddhartha awoke to the truth of the entire universe. He was thirty-five. In Japanese tradition the day of his enlightenment is held to be December 8 and is celebrated as his "attainment of buddhahood."

Q: What kind of life did Siddhartha lead after his awakening?

Once he attained his awakening, Siddhartha felt that what he had become aware of was so profound that even if he told it to others they would not be able to comprehend it. Therefore, he secretly decided to keep this profundity to himself.

However, perceiving this, Brahman (held to be the highest of all the gods) appeared before him, and entreated him to preach what he had awakened to in order to save people from incessant suffering.

Acceding to Brahman's words, he determined to preach and demonstrate the content of his own enlightenment and lead others to the same level of enlightenment. That is, he resolved to propagate the teachings in order to lead all living beings to awakening.

その後のシッダールタの人生は、まさにこの
伝道のためにささげた一生でした。自分を慕っ
て集まる弟子たちに真理を説き、また巷で厳し
い現実に苦しむ人たちに教えを説いて、心の救
済を果たそうとしたのです。そのような伝道の
生活は、彼が80歳でこの世を去るまで、休むこ
となく続けられました。

シッダールタは、悟りを開いた後、出身部族
であるシャークヤ族の聖者という意味で「シャ
ークヤ・ムニ」と呼ばれました。中国ではこれ
を「釈迦牟尼」と音写したのです。これが短縮
されて、中国や日本では「釈迦」と呼ばれるよ
うになりました。

Q: 釈迦の弟子になったのはどんな人たちですか？

釈迦は、初め、5人の苦行者仲間を教化する
ことにしました。そこでバーラーナシーの町に
ある仙人たちの修行所を訪れました。

5人は最初、苦行を捨てた釈迦を単なる堕落
者と見ていましたが、釈迦の崇高な姿に打た
れ、さらに彼の教えを聞いて感動し、弟子にな
ってしまいます。5人はほどなくして悟りを
得、6人の「阿羅漢」ができたと経典は伝えて
います。「阿羅漢」とは「アルハット」という
古代インド語を音写した言葉で、「供養を受け
るに値する人」を意味したものです。

その後、釈迦は町の長者の息子ヤシャスをは
じめその友人54人を教化し、弟子としました。

また、マガダ国には火の神に仕えるカーシャ
パという名の3人の兄弟がいて、彼らは1000人
もの弟子を抱える大物でした。ところが釈迦
は、神通力で彼らを教化して、そのすべてを弟

From that point on, his life was truly devoted to this mission. He preached the truth to the disciples who devotedly gathered around him and preached the teachings at the crossroads to those who suffered from the harshness of reality, attempting to accomplish salvation of the mind. He continued his preachings without interval until he left this world at the age of eighty.

After he attained enlightenment, he came to be known as *Sakya-muni,* sage of the Sakyas, after the name of his tribe. The Chinese transliterated this as *Shakamuni,* and this was shortened in China and Japan to simply *Shaka,* meaning "The Buddha."

Q: What kinds of people became the Buddha's disciples?

At the beginning, the Buddha decided to awaken his five companion ascetics. He therefore visited the practice hall of the hermits at Baranasi.

At first, these five looked upon the Buddha who had failed in his ascetic practices as a mere fallen monk, but affected by his dignity and moved by his teachings, they became disciples. Soon afterward they too attained enlightenment, and the scriptures tell us that six *arhats* were manifested. *Arhat* is an Indian word meaning "one who is worthy of receiving obeisance."

The Buddha later preached to Yasas, son of a wealthy merchant in that town, and fifty-four of his friends and they all became disciples.

In the kingdom of Magadha lived three renowned brothers named Kasyapa who worshipped the [Brahman] god of fire and whose entourage numbered a thousand disciples. The Buddha converted them with his divine powers and their disci-

子としてしまいました。ここに仏教は大教団へ
の道を歩くことになるのです。

　さらにその後、教団の中核となる「十大弟
子」と呼ばれる優秀な人材が釈迦の弟子として
加わり、教団を大きく発展させていくことにな
ります。

　なお、故郷の釈迦国の人々もおおぜい入団し
ました。釈迦の義母のマハー・プラジャーパテ
ィーや妻のヤショーダラーなども出家し、初め
て尼僧集団が成立しました。さらに、釈迦や弟
子のための僧坊である祇園精舎を寄進したス
ダッタ長者をはじめ、商人や王侯貴族など多く
の在家の信者が外から教団を支えてくれるよう
になりました。

Q: 釈迦はいくつまで生き、どのようにして亡くなったのですか？

　永い伝道生活を続け、80歳になった釈迦は、
侍者のアーナンダを連れて老いた身をかばいな
がら故郷へ旅立ちました。そして途中パーヴァ
ーの村に着いた時、鍛冶屋のチュンダが供養を
申し出て釈迦はこれを受けます。

　釈迦はこの時出されたスーカラ・マッダヴァ
という食べ物を食べて「血のほとばしる病」に
かかり、老いた身がいっそう衰弱してしまいま
した。釈迦の活動を書いた経典では、この食べ
物をきのこといっていますが、豚肉という説も
あり、はっきりしません。

　このあと釈迦は、アーナンダとともにクシナ
ガラまで行き、シャーラ樹の林に身を横たえて
亡くなるのです。このシャーラ樹は「沙羅双

ples became his own. At this juncture, Buddhism set forth on the path to becoming a major religious group.

Following that, certain esteemed followers who became known as the "Ten Great Disciples" became central figures in this religious group, and the group of followers developed and grew larger.

Large numbers of people from the Buddha's homeland also joined the order. His foster mother Mahaprajapati and his wife Yasodhara also renounced the world, forming the first order of priestesses. Moreover, support for the group began to come from outside the order, from such laypersons as merchants, members of royalty and the wealthy Sudatta who contributed the Jetavana-vihara priests' quarters for the Buddha and his disciples.

Q: **How long did the Buddha live and how did he die?**

Having continued a long lifetime of propagation and having reached the age of eighty, the Buddha set out with his companion Ananda for home, taking due consideration of his frail constitution. Along the way they passed through the village of Pava, where the lay believer Chunda, a smith, requested permission to offer the Buddha a meal, an offering which was accepted.

Upon eating the meal called Sukara-maddava that was served, the Buddha came down with severe indigestion, and his already weakened condition grew even worse. The scriptures that report the Buddha's activities say the food in question was made of a certain mushroom, but other traditions say it was pork, and there is no clarity on this issue.

Accompanied by Ananda, the Buddha then made his way to Kusinagara, where he lay on his side in a grove of sala trees and died. This grove of sala appears in the passage at the

樹」と音写され、『平家物語』の冒頭の、「祇園
精舎の鐘の声、諸行無常の響きあり、沙羅双樹
の花の色、盛者必衰の理をあらわす」という
言葉で知られています。

　これは釈迦が80歳、2月15日のことだったと
伝えられ、今でもこの日を「涅槃会」と呼んで
法会が行われています。

Q: 釈迦が亡くなった時、どんな遺言を残したのでしょうか?

　後代の伝承では、釈迦が亡くなった時、神々
や天女たち、多くの人々、また動物たちもが集
まって、その死を悲しんだといいます。

　釈迦の最後の旅に関する記録は、当時の大衆
的な言葉であったパーリ語で伝わる南方仏教の
大般涅槃経というお経に詳しく記されていま
す。

　それによると、釈迦は亡くなる前、まず、自
分はなにひとつ隠すことなく、自分の悟りの内
容のすべてを弟子たちに伝えていることを宣言
しています。このことは、これが釈迦の伝道の
姿勢であり、また秘儀をもって教団を支配する
ような意図がまったくなかったことを示してい
ると思われます。

　また、釈迦は自分の葬儀は在家の信者に任
せ、弟子は怠らずに修行に励むようにと諭して
います。そして自分亡きあと、僧として弟子た
ちがどのように生きるべきかを説き聞かせまし
た。

　伝承によると、釈迦は弟子たちに、自分が亡
くなったあとは「みずからを灯明(島)とし、
みずからを帰依処となせ。法を灯明(島)と
し、法を帰依処となせ」と教えています。この

beginning of *The Tale of the Heike* which mentions the bell of the Gion Temple and the faded flowers of the sala trees at the Buddha's deathbed.

It is said that he died at the age of eighty on February fifteenth. On the anniversary of this day a Buddhist service called *Nehan'e* is still held each year.

Q: What were the parting words of the Buddha?

In the oral tradition created years later it is said that when the Buddha died, the gods, celestial maidens and large numbers of people and animals gathered together and mourned his death.

The record of the Buddha's final journey is given in great detail in Pali, the commonly used language, in a sutra of Southern Buddhism known as *The Sutra of the Great Extinction*.

According to this, the Buddha declared before he died that he had transmitted the entirety of his enlightenment to his disciples, keeping absolutely nothing from them. This can be taken as the Buddha's stance in propagation and indicates that he had absolutely no intention of exercising control over the religious order by means of secret doctrines.

The Buddha admonished his disciples to continue their practices without lapsing and to leave arrangements for his own funeral to lay believers. He then preached to them concerning how they ought to live as priests following his death.

According to tradition, he taught them that following his death they must "be lights unto themselves and rely upon themselves alone, and make the Law their light, relying upon it and nothing else." This teaching of "Make the self your light,

教えは「自灯明・法灯明」と呼ばれ、仏教の
核心をなす思想の1つとされています。

　そして、釈迦は人々に「なにか質問はない
か」と3度繰り返して問い、沈黙する人々に最
後にこう言ったといいます。「すべてのものは
移り変わり、過ぎ去ってしまう。だからこそ常
に怠らず、精進せよ」と。

make the Law your light" is held as a core idea in the Buddhist faith.

Then three times he asked those assembled there, "Have you anything to ask me?" and being met with silence, he left these last words: "All phenomena are constantly changing. Therefore always remain assiduous."

仏教の基本的な教え

The Essential Teachings of Buddhism

Q: 仏教とは、一口に言ってどういうものなのですか？

仏教とは、言うまでもなく仏の教えです。それは、キリスト教がイエス・キリストの教えであり、イスラム教がモハメッドの教えであるのと同じです。

ところが、仏教にはひとつ、仏教だけにしかない大きな特徴があります。それは、仏教を学ぶ私たちも仏になれるということです。キリスト教やユダヤ教、イスラム教などでは、教祖の教えを学び、唯一絶対の神へ帰依することを勧めますが、人間が神になることができるとは言いません。

2

Q: In a nutshell, what is Buddhism?

Buddhism is the teachings of the Buddha, just as Christianity is the teachings of Jesus Christ and Islam is the teachings of Mohammed.

Yet there is one major characteristic that is unique to Buddhism, and this is that those who embrace Buddhism can also become Buddhas. In Christianity, Judaism and Islam, believers are encouraged to learn the teachings of the founder and to devote themselves to a unique, absolute deity, but human beings cannot become a deity.

しかし、仏教では仏の教えを学び、宇宙や人間に関する真理を悟ることによって、だれしもが仏になれるというのです。そのようにして、究極的にみんなが仏になることを目指すのが仏教であると言えます。

Q: なぜ釈迦を「仏」と呼ぶのですか？

インドの言葉で、「目覚めた者」のことを「ブッダ」といいます。釈迦は6年間に及ぶ苦行の後、苦行に見切りをつけ、今度は菩提樹の下で瞑想に入りますが、その瞑想で、ついに真理を発見しました。そのため、人々は「真理に目覚めた人」という意味で、釈迦のことを「ブッダ」と呼ぶようになりました。

やがて仏教は西域を経て中国に受け入れられますが、中国の人々はこの「ブッダ」という言葉を漢字で「仏陀」と音写しました。この言葉がそのまま日本に伝わり、日本では上の1字の「仏」だけをとって、「ぶつ」とか「ほとけ」と呼び習わすようになったのです。

Q: 釈迦以外にも仏と呼ばれる人はいるのですか？

釈迦以外にも宇宙の真実を悟り、真理に目覚める人がいても不思議ではありません。まず、釈迦が亡くなって間もなく、釈迦がこの世に生まれる以前にも、真理に目覚めた7人の仏がいたとされました。これらの仏は「過去七仏」と呼ばれて、人々に信仰されるようになりました。

また後には、未来にも、真理に気づき仏となるものが出現するという考えが生まれ、未来仏

The Essential Teachings of Buddhism Q&A 43

However, in Buddhism, by learning the teachings of the Buddha, and awakening to the truth concerning the universe and human beings, anyone is said to be able to become a buddha. Hence it can be said that ultimately Buddhism is everyone's attempting to become such a buddha.

Q: Why is the Buddha also called *hotoke*?

In an Indian language, the word for an "aspirant" is *buddha*. After practicing austerities for six years, the Buddha forsook these severe practices, began to meditate under a bo tree, and eventually discovered the truth. For that reason, people began to call him "Buddha" in the sense of "one who has awakened to the truth."

At some later time, as the teachings came to be received in the western regions of Asia and were received by China, the Chinese used two characters (*butsu* and *da*) for the word *buddha*. When this two-character name was transmitted into Japan, the first character was the only one used, and it came to be read as both *butsu* and *hotoke*.

Q: Is there anyone other than the Buddha who is called a buddha?

It would not be strange if someone other than the Buddha were to realize the true nature of the universe and attain awareness of its truths. Not long after the Buddha died, it was determined that there had been seven others who had awakened to the truth. They came to be called "the past seven buddhas" and people came to venerate them.

Later it was held that in the future others would become aware of the truth and become buddhas, and there developed

として信仰の対象となりました。その代表が、今から56億7000万年後にこの世に現れて人々を救うといわれる「弥勒仏（みろくぶつ）」です。

そして、釈迦が亡くなってから弥勒仏がこの世に現れるまでの間の人々の救済を釈迦に委託されたのが、地蔵菩薩です。日本では「お地蔵さん」として庶民に親しまれています。菩薩とは、人々を救いつつ、仏になることを目指して修行する人のことです。

これで、過去から現在、そして未来を貫く時間の系の上に仏が想定され、私たちの祖先、現在に生きている私たち、そして私たちの子孫を救済してくれることが保証されることになったわけです。

ところで、宇宙は空間的にも無限です。そこで、この無限の宇宙にも多数の仏が存在すると考えられるようになりました。例えば、はるか西のかなたには極楽（ごくらく）という世界があり、そこで現在、阿弥陀仏（あみだぶつ）という仏が教えを説いているといわれています。

また、東のかなたには浄瑠璃世界（じょうるり）という国があり、薬師如来（やくしにょらい）が人々を導いているといいます。そのほかにも宇宙のあらゆる方角に多数の仏が想定されているのです。

阿弥陀仏
Amida Buddha

Q: 阿弥陀仏と言ったり阿弥陀如来と言ったりしますが、「仏」と「如来」とはどう違うのですか？

「仏」と「如来」は同じです。

「仏」とは「真理に目覚めた者」のことをいいます。一方、「如来」とは古代インドの「タターガタ」という言葉を漢訳したもので、「タター」（本来そうあるべき状態）＋「ガタ」（行く）、

another kind of faith in "the future buddhas." As a representative, Miroku Buddha is supposed to appear 5,670,000,000 years from now in order to save human beings.

Further, *Jizō Bosatsu* (the Bodhisattva Jizō) was entrusted by the Buddha with saving others between the time of the Buddha's demise and the arrival of Miroku. In Japan, *Jizō* is popular among ordinary people as *O-Jizō-sama*. A bodhisattva (*bosatsu*) continues saving others who are practicing to become a buddha.

Therefore, on the supposition that there are buddhas along the axis of time from past to present and into the future, our own ancestors, those of us who are alive now, and our own descendants are guaranteed salvation.

The universe itself is infinite, and it came to be felt that in this unlimited universe there must exist a number of buddhas. For example, far to the West is a world called paradise, and it is said that in this land of supreme happiness the Buddha Amida is now preaching the teachings.

In the east is the Pure Lapis-Lazuli World, a land where people are guided by Yakushi Nyorai. In addition to these, it is believed that in all quarters of the universe are a large number of buddhas.

Q: People sometimes say Amida Buddha and Amida Tathagata, but what exactly is the difference between "buddha" and "tathagata"?

"Buddha" and "Tathagata" are one and the same.

"Buddha" means "one who has awakened to truth." The Sino-Japanese compound word "Nyorai" comes from an Indian word *tathagata*, meaning *tatha* (the condition of being as it should be) and *gata* (going), or perhaps *agata* (coming).

または「タター」＋「アーガタ」（来る）という合成語といわれています。

中国人は、そのうちの「来る」のほうに力点を置いて「如来」と訳したのでしょう。

本来あるべき状態を示す「タター」（正式には接尾語のtāがついて「タタター」）は「真如」とも訳され、悟りの世界、絶対真理の世界を表します。宗教的な理想の世界と考えていいでしょう。「真理に目覚めた者」という時の「真理」も同じことです。

ですから「如来」とは、「絶対真理の世界から来て衆生を救済するもの」というほどの意味で、仏の働きの側面に焦点を当てて呼んだ異名なのです。釈迦仏を釈迦如来、阿弥陀仏を阿弥陀如来、などと言い換えても、その意味はまったく同じということです。

Q:「涅槃」とはどんなことですか？

「涅槃」とは、古代インドの「ニルヴァーナ」または「ニッヴァン」という言葉の音写で、「火を吹き消した状態」を意味します。荒れ狂う執着や欲望の火が吹き消され、静かで穏やかになった心境を表しています。

一方、「悟り」とは、釈迦が瞑想の中で論理的に究明していって把握した真理でした。釈迦はその場で自分が悟った内容に従い、みずからの心の中の執着や欲望と戦いました。そして燃え盛るこれらの火を吹き消し、苦を離れた静寂な心境を獲得したのです。これが涅槃の境地です。

「悟り」がどちらかというと論理的なイメージを持っていたのに対し、「涅槃」は情緒的なイメージを持つといえるかもしれません。一般

The Chinese laid stress on the sense of "coming," thus leading to the current characters for *nyorai* in Japanese.

The word *tatha* indicating the original condition of something was also translated as *shinnyo*, meaning "thusness" and representing the world of enlightment, the world of Absolute Truth. This is what is meant by truth in the expression "one who has awakened to the truth."

Therefore, *tathagata* (*nyorai*) has the meaning of "one who has come from the world of absolute truth in order to save all sentient beings." It is therefore another name for "buddha" which places special emphasis on the workings of the buddha. Whether one refers to Sakya Buddha or Sakya Tathagata, the meaning is absolutely identical.

Q: What is "nirvana"?

The Japanese word *Nehan* is a transliteration of the Indian words *nirvana* or *nibbana*, meaning "the state of a flame being blown out." It represents the quiet, refreshing state of mind that exists when the fires of raging attachment and desire are extinguished.

On the other hand, "enlightenment" is the truth that the Buddha grasped during meditation by logical inquiry. In accordance with the contents of his enlightenment, the Buddha struggled against the attachments and the desires in his own mind. Extinguishing this vigorously burning flame, he achieved a tranquil state of mind separated from suffering. This is the realm of nirvana.

So it may be said that "enlightenment" possesses a somewhat logical nuance, whereas "nirvana" seems rather more emotional. In general usage, enlightenment and nirvana can be

に、悟りと涅槃はほとんど同じ意味と考えられていますが、ほんとうはその両方を身につけてこそ真の悟りといえるのでしょう。

また、「火を吹き消した状態」の火とは、「生命の火」と考えることもできます。だから、「涅槃」は死を意味することもあります。現に、釈迦の死は「完全な涅槃」という意味で「大般涅槃(だいはつねはん)」とも呼ばれています。

Q: 「解脱(げだつ)」とはどんなことですか?

インドでは古代から、あらゆる生き物は死んではまた別の存在に生まれ変わり、何度も生死を繰り返すと信じられてきました。これを「輪廻(りんね)」、または「輪廻転生(りんねてんしょう)」と呼びます。仏教でもこの考えを踏襲していて、生きとし生けるものは次の6つの世界に生存を繰り返すとしました。

(1) 天道(てんどう)……快楽に満ちた天人の世界。

(2) 人道(にんどう)……私たち人間の世界。

(3) 阿修羅道(あしゅらどう)……怒りに満ちた魔の世界。

(4) 畜生道(ちくしょうどう)……家畜や動物の世界。

(5) 餓鬼道(がきどう)……常に飢えに苦しむ世界。

(6) 地獄道(じごくどう)……拷問にさいなまれる最悪の世界。

これら6つの世界を「六道(ろくどう)」といい、あらゆる生き物はこの六道を転々と生まれ変わるので、輪廻は「六道輪廻(ろくどうりんね)」とも呼ばれます。

この六道はいずれも苦の世界です。天道でさえも、最後には老いと死を迎えなければならない苦しみの世界なのです。快楽が多い分、その苦しみは悲惨を極めるとさえ言われます。

thought of as having the same meaning, and to have truly attained both is to have achieved true awakening.

Further, one can take the "flame" of "the state of a flame being extinguished" as referring to "the flame of life." Therefore, nirvana can also have the meaning of death. As a matter of fact, the death of the Buddha is referred to as "the Great Extinction," in the sense of "absolute nirvana."

Q: What is "emancipation"?

In India since ancient times it has been believed that when all living things die, they are reborn as a separate existence and that they experience this rebirth again and again. This is called "transmigration" or "reincarnation." Buddhism followed this belief, saying that all sentient beings existed and were reborn in the "six states of existence":

(1) the way of *devas*—the realm of heavenly beings filled with pleasure
(2) the way of human beings—the human realm
(3) the way of *asuras*—the realm of evil filled with anger
(4) the way of animals—the realm of animals and livestock
(5) the way of *pretas*—the realm of hungry spirits
(6) the way of beings in hell—the worst realm wracked by torture

Because all sentient beings are reborn consecutively within these "six paths," "transmigration" is also called "reincarnation within the six realms."

Each of these six belongs to the world of suffering. Even the realm of the devas is a world of suffering in which one ultimately has to grow old and die. It is even said that because there is greater pleasure, it increases the misery of the suffering.

私たちは地球を回り続ける人工衛星のように、苦を中心にした六道を生き死にしつつ周回しているわけですが、衛星が地球の引力を解放されて、宇宙に脱出するように、私たちも六道輪廻から脱出しなければなりません。

脱出するためには、修行を積んで涅槃に入るか、浄土に往生して修行し、悟りを開くしかありません。この六道輪廻から脱出することを「解脱」というのです。それで結果的に解脱は悟りに結びつきます。だから「悟り」「涅槃」「解脱」という3つの言葉は同義語のように考えられているのです。

Q: 「悟り」とはどんなことですか?

「悟り」とは古代インドの「ボーディ」という言葉の意訳で、ボーディは「菩提」と音写されます。だから、「悟り」と「菩提」は同じ意味です。宇宙や人間の構造・道理を身をもって知ることといえるでしょう。

釈迦は、人間とは本来苦しみを背負った存在だと考えました。人間はだれしもいつかは年老い、病気になって死ななければなりません。それは苦しみです。また、愛する人ともいつかは別れなければならず、欲しいものはなかなか手に入りません。それもまた苦しみです。

では、私たちはなぜそのように苦しまなければならないのでしょうか。それは、人間が欲望や執着を持つからです。必ず死ななければならない存在なのに生に執着し、また次々と欲望を膨らませていくから自分の思いどおりにならず、人間は苦しむのです。

私たちがそのような苦しみから解放されるためには、どうすればいいのでしょうか。釈迦

Like a man-made satellite which circles the globe, we go round the six realms of existence pulled by the core of suffering. Just as a satellite may escape from the gravity of the earth and escape into space, we too must gain emancipation from the six realms of transmigration.

To do this, one must either accumulate practices and enter nirvana, or be reborn in the Pure Land, practice there, and achieve enlightenment. This release from the reincarnation within the six realms is called "emancipation." In effect, emancipation is tied with enlightenment and the three words enlightenment, nirvana, and emancipation are taken as synonymous.

Q: What is "enlightenment"?

Enlightenment, or *satori*, is a translation of the Indian word *bodhi*, which is transliterated as *bodai* in Japanese, hence enlightenment and *bodai* are synonymous. This is the absolute understanding of the composition and the truths of the universe and human beings.

The Buddha thought that human beings are originally beings which bear suffering. Every human eventually has to grow old, experience illness, and die. That is suffering. One has to part from who one loves and may be unable to obtain what one wants. This, too, is suffering.

Why is it that we must suffer in this way? It is because human beings have desires and attachments. Humans suffer because they grow attached to life despite the fact that they have to die, and because their desires expand from one to another and they are unable to attain satisfaction.

How are we to be released from such suffering? The Buddha thought that since attachment and desire were the causes of

は、苦しみの原因は執着や欲望にあるのだか
ら、その執着や欲望を捨て去れば（またはコン
トロールすれば）、苦しみもまたなくなると考
えました。そして彼は、執着や欲望をコントロ
ールする修行法を考案したのです。

　釈迦は菩提樹の下で坐禅を組み、瞑想に入り
ました。そしてこのような人間の心の構造と宇
宙の道理を体得し、真理に目覚めました。この
体験を「悟り」といい、「菩提」と呼ぶのです。

Q: 釈迦が悟ったこととはどんなことだったのですか？

　一口には答えることができない質問です。な
ぜならば、8万4000もあるといわれる仏の教え、
現在に伝えられている膨大な経典すべてが、釈
迦の悟りの内容と言えるからです。

　しかし、あえてその中の代表的なものを選ん
でみることにしましょう。

(1) 四諦……苦しみとその原因、および苦し
　　みを滅すること、その滅に至る方法に関す
　　る4つの真理。

(2) 八正道……苦の原因を滅する8つの方
　　法。

(3) 十二因縁……老死に至る苦の原因を12段
　　階にわたって考察した真理。

(4) 中道……苦行や快楽などの極端な方法に
　　よって悟りを得ることはできず、中道を歩
　　むべきだということ。

　その一つ一つについては、次に少し詳しく説
明しましょう。

suffering, if we could cast attachment and desire aside (or at least control them), suffering would also disappear. He also conceived a means of practice whereby one could control attachment and desire.

The Buddha seated himself beneath the bodhi tree and entered meditation. He comprehended the makeup of the human mind and the nature of the universe and awakened to the truth. This experience is called "enlightenment" (*satori*) and is referred to as *bodai*.

Q: What was it that the Buddha awakened to?

It is impossible to answer this in a few words. This is because the vast number of scriptures which contain the teachings of the Buddha—and which are said to number 84,000— can all be said to be the contents of that enlightenment.

Yet let us try to select the most representative among them.

(1) The Four Noble Truths —- The four truths concerning suffering, its causes, the extinguishing of it and the means of extinguishing that suffering.

(2) The Eightfold Noble Path —- The eight means by which one eliminates the causes of suffering.

(3) The Twelve Causes —- The truth which explains the twelve-stage factors of suffering leading to old age and death.

(4) The Middle Path —- One cannot attain enlightenment through the extremes of austerities or pleasures, but only by walking in the Middle Path.

Next, let's look at each of these in more detail.

Q:「四諦」とはどんなことですか?

「諦」とは「明らめる」、つまり真理を明らか
にすることで、「四諦」とは「4つの真理」と
いう意味。その4つとは次の通りです。
 (1) 苦諦……この世は苦であるという真理。

 (2) 集諦……苦には原因があるという真理。
 (3) 滅諦……原因を滅すれば苦もまた滅する
  という真理。
 (4) 道諦……そのための適切な方法を示した
  真理。
「四諦」を理解するために、病気を例にとっ
て考えてみましょう。

私たちは病気という苦に苦しんでいます。こ
の現実が「苦諦」です。病気には原因がありま
す。これが「集諦」です。その原因を除去すれ
ば病気は治ります。これが「滅諦」に相当しま
す。そして、そのために適切な処置を行う必要
があるとして示された処方箋が「道諦」で、釈
迦はこの治療法を実践することを勧めたので
す。

このように、四諦は医学における論理展開と
似ているため、この論理を説いた釈迦は「医
王」とも呼ばれました。

Q:「八正道」とはどんなことですか?

四諦のうちの道諦、つまり苦の原因をなくす
ための方法として、8種類の修行法があげられ
ています。これが「八正道」で、次の8つで
す。
 (1) 正見……正しい見解。
 (2) 正思惟……正しい考え。

Q: What are the Four Noble Truths (*shitai*)?

The character *tai* of the word *shitai* means "to make clear," that is, "to make the truth clear." The four truths which are elucidated are as follows.

(1) The Truth of Suffering — The truth that this is a world of suffering.

(2) The Truth of Cause — The truth that suffering has cause.

(3) The Truth of Extinction — The truth that when cause is extinguished, so is suffering.

(4) The Truth of the Path — The truth of the proper way to achieve this.

In order to understand the Four Noble Truths, let us take the example of illness.

Being afflicted with the suffering of illness is "The Truth of Suffering." The cause of the illness is "The Truth of Cause." If the cause is eliminated, the illness will be cured. This is "The Truth of Extinction." The prescription that is issued as an appropriate measure to be taken is "The Truth of the Path," and the Buddha encourages us to actually practice this method of treatment.

Because the Four Noble Truths resemble the logical development of medical science, the Buddha who preached this logic is also called "the king of medicine."

Q: What is the Eightfold Noble Path?

There are eight varieties of actual practice which are indicated as means by which one can carry out the Truth of the Path, which is included among the Four Noble Truths. They are as follows:

(1) *shōken* — right view

(2) *shōshiyui* — right thinking

（3）正語……正しい言葉。
（4）正業……正しい行い。
（5）正命……正しい生活。
（6）正精進……正しい努力。
（7）正念……正しい注意。
（8）正定……正しい禅定。

上の6番目までは、「よこしまな物の見方を
しない」「よこしまな考えを起こさない」「よこ
しまな言葉を使わない」というように、邪悪な
行為を排する修行と考えたほうがわかりやすい
かもしれません。

それに対して7番目と8番目は、積極的に心
を鍛えていく修行になるわけです。これらを日
常実践していくことによって、苦の原因となる
執着や欲望をコントロールするのです。

Q:「十二因縁（十二縁起）」とはなんですか？

釈迦は、苦の原因を「四諦」の論理で解き明
かしました。この時、彼はもう1つ、老死とい
う苦しみの原因を、別の論理で解明したといわ
れています。老死自体はだれも避けられないの
ですが、そこから来る人間の憂いや悲しみなど
という苦悩の原因を、釈迦は追求したのです。

憂いや悲しみの原因は、人間が必ず年老い、
死んでしまうという運命を背負っているからで
す。では、老死の原因とはなんでしょうか。そ
れはこの世に生を受けることから生じます。で
は生を受けるのはなぜ。それは、輪廻によって
六道を生まれ変わるからです。

このようにして順番に原因をたどっていき、
12段階目に、釈迦は、最終的な「無明」という
根本原因に行き着いたのです。「無明」という
のは無知、真実がわからないことを言います。

(3) *shōgo* —- right speech
(4) *shōgō* —- right action
(5) *shōmyō* —- right living
(6) *shōshōjin* —- right endeavor
(7) *shōnen* —- right memory
(8) *shōjō* —- right meditation

The first six, in the sense of "do not have wicked views," "do not give rise to wicked thoughts," and "do not employ wicked language," can perhaps best be thought of as practices to eliminate wicked acts.

In contrast, the seventh and eighth are practices for positively disciplining the mind. By actually practicing these day by day, one becomes able to control the attachments and desires which cause suffering.

Q: What is the Law of the Twelve Causes?

The Buddha clarified the causes of suffering in the Four Noble Truths. It is said that on the same occasion he explicated a separate logic concerning the causes of the sufferings of aging and death. No one is able to escape from aging and death itself, but the Buddha probed the causes of the distress and sadness that afflict human beings as a result of them.

The cause of distress and sadness comes to the human fate of inevitably growing old and dying. What then is the cause of aging and death? It arises from having been given life in this world. And why is one given life? This is because of the cycle of rebirths in the six realms of transmigration.

The Buddha followed these causes in order and at the twelfth stage he arrived at the fundamental cause, an ultimate cause he called *mumyō*, meaning ignorance and not understanding truth. It stands to reason that if one were able to elim-

この「無明」という無知をなくすことができれ
ば、苦もまたなくなる、という道理が成立する
わけです。この、老死の原因を順番にたどって
いって無明に至る12の段階を、「十二因縁」ま
たは「十二縁起」というのです。

Q: 十二因縁の12の段階とはどんなものなのでしょうか?

十二因縁の一つ一つの内容を、根本原因であ
る無明のほうからたどっていくと、次のように
なります。

(1) 無明（むみょう）……無知であることです。真実がわ
からないことをいいます。

(2) 行（ぎょう）……行為のことです。無明（無知）に
基づいた行為をいいます。

(3) 識（しき）……認識のことです。無明（無知）に
基づく行為によって得る間違った認識をい
います。

(4) 名色（みょうしき）……認識の対象で、物質および感覚
器官を含みます。

(5) 六入（ろくにゅう）……認識する対象を知る感覚器官を
いいます。眼・耳・鼻・舌・身・意の6つ
を指します。

(6) 触（しょく）……外界との接触をいいます。六入に
よって名色（認識の対象）を感受し、外界
と接することです。

(7) 受（じゅ）……感受作用をいいます。外界と接触
することによって起きます。

(8) 愛（あい）……渇愛したり嫌悪したりすることを
いいます。感受したものを欲したり嫌った
りする作用です。

(9) 取（しゅ）……執着のことです。欲したり嫌った
りしたものに執着することです。

inate this ignorance, then suffering too would be extinguished. Following the order of causes leading to death from old age, and ultimately leading to ignorance, these twelve steps are referred to as the Twelve Causes or Twelve Causations.

Q: What are the twelve stages in the Law of the Twelve Causes?

The stages or links in the chain of the Twelve Causes are as follows, beginning with the fundamental cause of ignorance.

(1) *mumyō* —- Ignorance. Not being aware of truth.

(2) *gyō* —- Actions. Activity based on ignorance.

(3) *shiki* —- Consciousness. Mistaken consciousness based upon actions that arise from ignorance.

(4) *myō-shiki* —- Objects of consciousness, including both material objects and the organs of sense.

(5) *rokunyū* —- "Six entrances." Sense organs by which we know objects of consciousness. Indicates the six "organs" of the eye, ear, nose, tongue, body and mind.

(6) *shoku* —- Contact with external objects. The reception of the objects of consciousness by means of the "six entrances" and encounter with the outside world.

(7) *ju* —- Sensation. That which occurs via contact with external objects.

(8) *ai* —- Desiring pleasure and hatred. The function of either desiring or detesting the object of sensation.

(9) *shu* —- Clinging. Positive or negative attachment to what one desires or detests, respectively.

(10) 有……輪廻する生存のあり方です。そ
れは取（執着）によって生じます。

(11) 生……輪廻により、六道に生まれるこ
とです。

(12) 老死……文字通り、老いて死ぬことです。
輪廻で生まれ変わることによって、人はこ
の老死の苦を味わわなければなりません。

Q: 「無常」とはどういうことですか？

あらゆるものは「生滅変化する」（生まれ、
変化し、死ぬ）という、仏教の基本認識の１つ
です。これを「諸行無常」ともいいます。絶対
不変で、永遠に存続するものなどはありえない
といっているのです。

私たちの体を見ても、瞬間瞬間に多くの細胞
が死滅し、同時に多くの細胞が生まれて新陳代
謝を繰り返しています。そして、やがて私たち
の個体は死に至ります。無限に見える大宇宙で
すらも常に変化し、いつかは滅するでしょう。

ところが、私たちは今の状態がいつまでも続
くと錯覚しがちです。そのためにさまざまな誤
認を犯し、真実を見誤りがちです。そこで仏教
では、無常という真理を見据えて、物事を正し
く判断することを説いているのです。

Q: 「無我」とはどういうことですか？

永遠不変の絶対的な存在としての我などとい
うものはないということです。「無常」と似て
おり、２つは切り離せない思想ですが、無常で
はあらゆるものは生滅変化する、というところ
に力点が置かれているのに対して、無我では、

(10) *u* — The state of existence in transmigration. Arises from attachment.

(11) *shō* — Birth. Being born in the six realms by cause and effect.

(12) *rōshi* — Old age and death. Due to the law of causation, humans must experience the suffering of growing old and dying.

Q: What is impermanence?

The belief that all things arise, change, and die is one of the fundamental understandings of Buddhism. This is often expressed as "all things are impermanent." What this means is that nothing exists forever and absolutely unchanged.

Even in our own bodies, there are a large number of cells dying each moment, and at the same time they are being replaced by numerous new cells. Eventually our individual bodies arrive at death. Even the universe which appears to be infinite is forever transforming and will one day be extinguished.

However, we tend to live under the illusion that the present state of affairs will continue forever. As a result, we make various mistaken perceptions and misunderstand the truth. Buddhism teaches us to fix our eyes upon the truth of impermanence and to form a correct judgment about all things.

Q: What is "nothing has an ego"?

This means that there is no ego or self which is an absolute existence and remains unchanged forever. It is similar to "impermanence" and the two concepts are inseparable. "Impermanence" places emphasis on the truth that everything arises, changes and extinguishes, while "nothing has an ego"

絶対永遠の存在の否定が強調されます。すべて
は無我であるという意味で「諸法無我」といわ
れます。

　釈迦が、直接、無我の思想を説いたのかとい
う点に関しては、疑問が出されています。経典
によると、釈迦は「我執をなくせ」と強調しま
した。我がもの、我がものと執着するところに
苦しみが生まれると考えたからです。この主張
が後に発展し、無我の思想を形成したのではな
いかといわれています。

Q: 仏教は「苦」を説くと聞きますが、なぜですか?

　釈迦は、この世は苦しみの世界だと認識しま
した。すべては無常であり、私たちはいつかは
年老い、病気にかかり、死ななければなりませ
ん。

　そのことを、私たちは憂い、悲しみ、苦痛だ
と感じるからです。そこで仏教では、生まれ、
老い、病み、死ぬことを、生きとし生けるもの
の根本的な苦しみととらえ、「四苦」と呼びま
す。整理すると次のようになります。
(1) 生
(2) 老
(3) 病
(4) 死
　やがて、四苦に次の4つが加えられました。
(5) 愛別離苦……愛するものともいつかは別
れなければならない苦しみ。
(6) 怨憎会苦……憎しみの対象とも顔を合わ
せなければならない苦しみ。
(7) 求不得苦……求めるものが手に入らない
苦しみ。
(8) 五陰盛苦……五陰とは心身のこと。心

stresses the negation of an absolute, eternal existence. Because everything is "without a self," it is said that "nothing has an ego."

There has appeared some doubt as to whether the Buddha actually directly preached the idea of selflessness. According to the scriptures, the Buddha stressed elimination of attachment to the self. This is because he held that suffering arises from the self's attachment to things. Therefore it is said that this emphasis was later developed and formed the idea of "no self."

Q: Why is it that Buddhism preaches "suffering"?

The Buddha was aware that this world is one of suffering. All things are impermanent; we will someday grow old, fall ill and have to die.

We feel this as distress, cause for grief and anguish. Buddhism takes the fact of being born, growing old, becoming ill, and dying as the fundamental sufferings of all sentient beings and calls this the "Four Sufferings." These four are:

(1) birth
(2) old age
(3) illness
(4) death

At a later time, four more were added:

(5) parting from those one loves

(6) having to meet those one hates

(7) not being able to have what one desires

(8) clinging to the five aggregates; sufferings of the mind and

身の苦しみ。

　四苦にこの4つが加えられて「八苦」と呼ばれ、ここから「四苦八苦」という日本語が生まれたのです。

Q: 「縁起」とは仏教の言葉なのですか?

　仏教の言葉です。「縁起」とは、「因縁生起」という言葉の2番目と4番目の文字を取って省略した言葉なのです。

　「因縁生起」とは、あらゆるものは「因」と「縁」から生じるという意味です。因とは結果を招く直接の原因、縁とはこれを補助する間接の原因のことをいいます。これを説明するのによく使われる例に、「花」があります。

　花は種をまくことによって芽が出て、開花します。ですから、種は花が咲く直接の原因、つまり「因」です。

　ところで、花は種だけでは育ちません。水もあげなければなりませんし、太陽に当てることも必要です。この場合の水や太陽が、花を開花させる間接的な原因、つまり「縁」に当たります。

　花が種という因と、水や太陽という縁によって花を咲かせるように、私たちを含めたあらゆる存在は単独で成り立っているわけではなく、いろいろな原因や条件によって成立しています。

　このように、すべての事象は無数の原因や条件が相互に関係し合って成り立っており、原因や条件が変われば事象も変化するということを「縁起」というのです。だからすべては生滅変化するし(無常)、絶対不変の存在はない(無我)ということにつながるのです。

body

These four added to the first four are called the Eight Sufferings (*hakku*), and from this comes the Japanese expression
shiku-hakku, meaning "in agony or distress."

Q: Does the word "origin" (*engi*) come from Buddhism?

Yes. The word *engi* is a shortened form, using the second
and fourth characters, of the four-character expression *in-nen-
shō-ki*.

The four-character phrase means that everything has a
cause and a condition. "Cause" (*in*) are the factors which
directly bring about a result, and "condition" (*en*) refers to factors which complement the direct factors. The example of a
flower is often used to explain this.

A flower blooms because seeds are planted and shoots
come forth. Therefore, the seed is the direct cause (*in*) for the
blooming of the flower.

However, flowers will not grow simply from seeds. They
must be given water and sunshine. In this instance, water and
sunlight are indirect factors causing the flower to bloom, and
are, in other words, "conditions" (*en*).

In the same way that a flower is made to bloom as a result
of the "cause" of the seed and the "conditions" of the water and
sunshine, all existences including ourselves are not realized
independently, but rather are materialized as a result of various
causes and conditions.

Hence all phenomena are manifested as a result of the
mutual relationship of innumerable causes and conditions.
Engi refers to the fact that when those causes and conditions
change, the phenomena too will change. Therefore, this is con-
nected to "impermanence" (all things arise, change, and are
extinguished) and "no self" (no existence is absolute and

Q:「因果応報」とはなんですか？

　「因果」とは原因と結果という意味で、ある原
因があれば、必ず、なんらかの結果を招くし、
ある結果はなんらかの原因があったから生じて
いる、という考え方です。

　私たちはなんらかの行為をします。その行為
は原因となって、やはりなんらかの結果を生じ
させます。この道理から、仏教では善い行為を
行えばそれが原因となって善い結果を生じる
し、悪いことをすれば悪い結果を招くと考えら
れました。これを「善因善果」「悪因悪果」と
いいます。だから仏教では善を勧め、悪を退け
るのです。

　「親の因果が子に報い」などという言葉があり
ますが、因果とはあくまでも自分の行為が原因
となって自分が受ける結果をいうのであり、こ
の言葉は、仏教でいう因果とは違った意味に使
われるようになったものといえます。

Q: 仏教で菩提樹が大事にされるのはなぜですか？

　釈迦がこの木の下で坐禅を組み、瞑想をして
悟りを開いたので、尊い悟りを象徴する木とし
て大事にされるのです。

　そもそもこの木は菩提樹という名前ではあり
ませんでした。釈迦がこの木の下で菩提、すな
わち悟りを得たから、菩提樹と呼ばれるように
なったのです。

　この木はもともとピッパラ樹といい、古来か
ら霊力のある木とされていました。クワ科に属

immutable).

Q: What is "karmic retribution"?

Inga, in the sense of cause and effect, is the idea that if there is a cause, it will always summon forth some kind of effect, and in reverse, every effect comes forth because of some cause.

We carry out some act. That act becomes a cause, and it gives rise to some sort of effect. From this logic Buddhism concluded that if one carries out an act of goodness, it will have a good effect, and if one carried out an evil act, it will have an evil effect. This is referred to as "good cause good effect" and "bad cause bad effect." Therefore, Buddhism promotes goodness and avoids evil.

There is a saying that the sins of the parent will be the retribution of the child, but "cause" is something that one brings about oneself and the "result" is something one receives oneself. Therefore, such sayings are clearly mistaken.

Q: Why is the bodhi tree made much of in Buddhism?

The *bodhi* (*bo*) tree is given particular significance in Buddhism because the Buddha sat under this tree to meditate and through contemplation attained enlightenment, and the tree is seen as symbolizing that precious awakening.

Originally the tree was not called a bodhi tree, but because the Buddha awakened to *bodhi* (*bodai*), enlightenment, beneath the tree, it later came to be called the bodhi tree.

It was earlier called a *pippala* tree, and from ancient times was held to possess spiritual powers. It belongs to the mul-

し、葉っぱはハート型をしています。実は球状
で、数珠に用いられます。

Q: 経典とはなんですか？

　　釈迦の教えを集大成した聖典のことです。釈
迦の教えは、真理を説き示した教理と、教団を
運営するために必要な規則とに分かれます。狭
い意味ではこの教理を「経」といい、規則を
「律」といいます。

　　一方、釈迦の死後弟子たちは師の教えをさま
ざまに研究し、解釈しますが、このような解釈
書を「論」といいます。この「経」と「律」と
「論」を合わせて「三蔵」と呼び、広い意味で
は三蔵を称して「経」または「経典」というの
です。

　　釈迦が亡くなった時、当時釈迦に代わって教
団を統率していたマハー・カーシャパという弟
子は、師の教えが散逸してしまうことを心配し
ました。そこで彼は阿羅漢の悟りを得た500人
の高弟を一堂に集め、釈迦の教えを整理して体
系化することにしました。経については釈迦の
侍者としていつも側に付き従っていたアーナン
ダに担当させ、釈迦の言葉を述べさせました。
そして、それをみんなで確認し合ったのです。

　　同様に、律についてはウパーリという弟子が
担当しました。いわば、経典の編集会議が開か
れたわけです。こうして釈迦の教えが体系化さ
れ、ここに初めて経典が成立したのです。

　　その後何度かこのような集まりがもたれ、経
典は次第に整理されつつ今日まで継承されてき
たわけです。

berry family and has a heart-shaped leaf. The seeds are spherical and are used in rosaries.

Q: What are sutras?

Sutras are scriptures in which are compiled the teachings of the Buddha. The teachings of the Buddha are divided into the doctrines of the truth which he preached and the rules necessary for the functioning of the order. In a narrow sense, the doctrines are referred to as sutras and the rules are called precepts.

Following the death of the Buddha, the disciples studied and interpreted the teachings of their teacher, and their interpretative volumes are referred to as commentaries. Together the sutras, precepts, and commentaries are called the "Three Stores" or "Three Baskets," and in a broad sense the Three Stores are referred to as sutras and scriptures.

At the time of the Buddha's death, the disciple Mahakasyapa, who had been put in charge of leading the order, worried that the preachings of the teacher might become scattered and lost. Therefore, he gathered together five hundred disciples who had attained arhat enlightenment and had them systematize the Buddha's teachings. For the sutras, the Buddha's constant companion Ananda was put in charge of reciting the sermons of the Buddha. The assembly then approved what they heard.

In the same fashion, the disciple Upali was put in charge of reciting the precepts. As it were, they held a scripture editorial meeting. In this manner, the teachings of the Buddha were unified and for the first time manifested as scriptures.

Similar gatherings were held at later dates, the scriptures continued to be arranged, and we today have taken them over.

仏教の発展と日本への伝来

The Development of Buddhism and Its Introduction to Japan

Q: インドに生まれた仏教は、どのように世界に伝わって
いきましたか?

釈迦が亡くなって 100 年ほどたったころ、仏
教教団は、律(僧尼が守るべき生活規律)の解
釈をめぐって、20 もの部派に分裂してしまいま
す。しかし、この分裂は仏教の衰退を意味した
わけではありません。それどころか、それぞれ
の部派が力を広げていったため、仏教全体とし
てはたいへんな勢いでインド中に広まっていっ
たのです。この時代を「部派仏教」の時代と言
います。

そのころ、全インドを統一したマウリア王朝

3

Q: How was Buddhism, which was born in India, transmitted to the world?

A century after the death of the Buddha, the Buddhist order had fragmented into some twenty different sects over the matter of interpretation of the precepts (ordinances which monks were to abide by). However, this dissension was not indicative of a decline in Buddhism. To the contrary, because each of the sects expanded its strength, Buddhism with a great surge spread throughout India. This period is referred to as the age of sectarian Buddhism.

At that juncture, King Asoka acceded to the throne of the

のアショーカ王が即位し、彼は仏教を保護し、その発展におおいに寄与しました。

　そのアショーカ王の息子のマヘーンドラはスリランカに渡り、出家して修行で悟りを得ることを目的とした保守的な仏教（上座部仏教）を伝えました。この上座部仏教がスリランカをはじめ東南アジア諸国に延々と伝えられ、現在に至っています。

　一方、仏教が限られた出家者のものになっていることに疑問を感じた人々を中心に、宗教改革運動が起こりました。そして、利他救済の立場から広く人間の平等の成仏を説く仏教（大乗仏教）がインド中に広まったのです。紀元1世紀ごろのことで、この大乗仏教が西域を経て中国に伝えられました。

　中国人は懸命にこれを摂取し、周知のように一大仏教文化を中国に形成したのです。

　4世紀には、朝鮮半島にも仏教は伝えられ、そして遅れること約160年、朝鮮半島を経て、538年にはついに我が国にも仏教が伝えられました。こうして仏教は、アジア全域を含む世界宗教へと発展していったのです。

Q: 大乗仏教と小乗仏教（上座部仏教）の違いを説明してください。

　アショーカ王はインドの各地に仏塔を建てました。そして、仏塔はしだいに、釈迦を慕う在家信者たちの礼拝の対象となっていきました。

Mauria kingdom which had unified all of India, and he served as guardian to Buddhism and contributed greatly to its development.

King Asoka's son Mahendra crossed over to Ceylon (Sri Lanka) and transmitted a conservative Buddhism (Theravada) which took as its purpose renouncing the world and carrying out practices to attain enlightenment. This Theravada Buddhism was transmitted to Sri Lanka as well as the other nations of Southeast Asia and continues there today.

Meanwhile, a religious reform movement developed, centering around those who felt some skepticism concerning the limiting of Buddhism to those who had taken orders. Moreover, Mahayana Buddhism was spreading across India preaching from the doctrine of *ritakyūsai* (emancipation through benefitting others) that all human beings were equally capable of becoming buddhas. In the first century (of the Western era), this Mahayana Buddhism crossed through the western regions of Asia and was transmitted to China.

The Chinese eagerly adopted it and, as is common knowledge, a Buddhist culture of great importance was formed in China.

In the fourth century Buddhism was transmitted to the Korean Peninsula, and about one hundred sixty years later, it was introduced to Japan in the year 538. This is how Buddhism developed as a world religion encompassing the entirety of Asia.

Q: Could you please explain the difference between Mahayana Buddhism and Hinayana (Theravada) Buddhism?

King Asoka of India constructed *stupas* in every region of India. Gradually these *stupas* became objects of veneration among the lay believers who followed the Buddha.

　しかし一方、仏教教団の各部派は、一般大衆の救済よりも、むしろ寺院に閉じこもって難解な教理の研究に明け暮れるようになっていきました。やがて、そのような風潮に反発が起こり、宗教改革運動が起こりました。その担い手は、仏塔を崇拝する在家の信者たちと、革新派の部派の僧たちでした。

　彼らは従来の出家をして修行をするという仏教を、自分だけが小さな船に乗って悟りの岸に渡ろうとするような利己的なもので、「小乗仏教」とでも呼ぶのがふさわしい劣った仏教だと非難しました。それに対して、自分たちは、大衆のすべてを大きな船に乗せ、そのすべての人々を悟りの岸に渡す「大乗仏教」だとして民衆の支持を得ていったのです。

　小乗仏教（部派仏教）は、あくまで自分の解脱のために自分で修行するので、これを「自利」といいます。これに対して大乗仏教は、他人を救済する「利他」の修行があってはじめて自利は完成すると主張しました。そして、あらゆる人が釈迦と同じ仏になれるのだとして、それを理想としたのです。

　したがって、小乗仏教と大乗仏教の大きな違いは「自利」と「利他」にあるといえましょう。

Q: 「菩薩」とはどんな人ですか？

　悟りを求める人のことを、古代インドの言葉で「ボーディサットヴァ」といいます。これを中国人は「菩提薩埵」と音写し、日本ではこの１字目と３字目をとって「菩薩」と略称したの

But meanwhile, the various Buddhist sects came to be less concerned about the salvation of the general populace than with secluding themselves in temples and devoting themselves to the study of difficult doctrines from morning to night. Before long, a reaction against this trend occurred and there arose a movement for religious reform. Those who brought forth the changes were the lay believers who venerated the stupas and priests of the reformist sects.

They criticized existing Buddhism, in which one renounced the world and carried out practices was self-interested, as if one were to get in a small boat and try to reach the shore of enlightment all by oneself. They criticized this as an inferior Buddhism worthy of being called Lesser-Vehicle Buddhism. In contrast, they obtained the support of the masses by proclaiming that theirs was Greater-Vehicle Buddhism which could put the masses on a great vessel and take them all across to the shore of enlightenment.

Lesser-Vehicle Buddhism (Hinayana Buddhism) involves practicing by oneself strictly for one's own emancipation, and this is called "benefitting self." Contrary to this, Greater-Vehicle Buddhism insisted it is only through "benefitting others" by saving the other that one can perfect "benefitting self." And it took as its ideal the belief that everyone is capable of becoming a buddha.

Accordingly, the great distinction between Greater-Vehicle and Lesser-Vehicle Buddhism is "benefitting self" and "benefitting others."

Q: What kind of person is a bodhisattva?

The Indian word for one who seeks enlightenment is "bodhi-sattva." The Chinese transliterated this into the four-character *bodaisatta*, and the Japanese took the first and third characters to make *bosatsu*.

です。

　ですから、菩薩とはもともと悟りを求める人のことをいうのですが、最初は悟りを開く前の釈迦の呼称として使われていました。釈迦は悟りを開いてブッダになりましたが、悟る以前はまだブッダではないわけですから、弟子や信者たちは悟る以前の釈迦を菩薩と呼んだのです。

　ところが、大乗仏教が起こると事情は一変します。大乗仏教ではだれもが仏になれると考えましたから、他人を救済し、自分も悟りを求めようと決心した人をすべて菩薩と呼ぶようになったのです。だから、あなたも私も、仏道を歩もうと決心すればみんなが菩薩なのです。

　ところで、大乗仏教ではもう１つの菩薩の概念が生まれました。迷いの世界にいる生き物は無限にいます。それらすべてを救ってから仏になろうとすれば、自分はいつまでたっても仏になれません。そこで、みずからその厳しい道を選び取り、生きとし生けるものを救済し続ける菩薩が考え出されたのです。それが観音、普賢、弥勒などの諸菩薩です。これらは仏に無限に近い菩薩たちです。

　以上を整理すると、菩薩には次の３種があることになります。

　（１）悟りを開く前の釈迦の呼称。
　（２）求道を決意した人々。
　（３）仏と同類の衆生救済の菩薩。

Q:「南無阿弥陀仏」とか「南無妙法蓮華経」とかいいますが、なんのことですか？

　「南無」とは、インドの「ナマス」という言葉の音写です。ナマスとはおじぎをすることで、

Therefore, while bodhisattva refers to someone who is seeking enlightenment, it was used as the name by which the Buddha was first called before he attained enlightenment. Once he awakened, he became "Buddha," but in referring to him before enlightenment, his disciples and believers called him "*bodhisattva.*"

With the appearance of Greater-Vehicle Buddhism a drastic change occurs. According to Greater-Vehicle Buddhism, anyone can become a buddha, so everyone who seeks to save others and achieve enlightenment oneself can be called a bodhisattva. Therefore, you and I as well as anyone else who decides to take the path of Buddhism are *bodhisattva.*

Within Greater-Vehicle Buddhism arose another concept of bodhisattva. There are an infinite number of living beings in the world of illusion. If one tried to save them all before becoming a buddha oneself, then one could never achieve buddhahood. There arose the concept of the bodhisattva who on his own chooses the austere path of continuing to try to save all sentient beings. These are the bodhisattva Kannon, Fugen and Miroku. These bodhisattva are infinitely close to buddhas.

In sum, there are three ways in which "bodhisattva" is used.
(1) The name of the Buddha before his awakening.
(2) Those who make up their minds to pursue the path.
(3) Bodhisattva identical to buddhas who seek to save all living beings.

Q: Why do people say *"Namu Amida Butsu"* and *"Namu Myōhō Renge-kyō"*?

"Namu" is the transliteration of the Indian word *"namasu,"* which is a bow and which is translated as "devotion" and

「帰依」とか「信従」などと訳されます。

したがって、「南無阿弥陀仏」といえば阿弥陀仏に帰依しますという意味で、「南無妙法蓮華経」といえば、『妙法蓮華経』（『法華経』と略称）というお経に帰依します、という意味になります。ほかにも「南無仏」「南無三宝」などと使われます。

Q: 大乗仏教の経典とはどんなものですか？

大乗仏教の経典は、紀元前後のころから作られはじめたと考えられています。だから釈迦が直接に説いたこととはいえません。しかし、釈迦の教えの原点に帰ろうとする大乗仏教徒たちが、瞑想によって釈迦の考えを再構築したものですから、それはやはり経典とされています。

大乗仏教経典は、後世に多大な思想的影響を与えました。その代表的なものを紹介しましょう。

・般若経

「般若」とは古代インドの「プラジュニャー」または「パンニャー」という言葉を音写したもので、「智慧」という意味です。智慧とは真理を知る力のことで、「知恵」とは区別されています。

「般若経」とは固有名詞ではなく、智慧を完成することによって悟ることを説く経典群の総称です。それには600巻に及ぶ『大般若経』や、『大品般若経』『小品般若経』などがあります。

『般若心経』は、それら膨大な般若経の真髄をわずか260余字で表したお経で、もっともポ

"compliance."

Accordingly, *"Namu Amida Butsu"* means that one believes in Amida. *"Namu Myōhō Renge-kyō"* means that one believes in the *Sutra of the Lotus of the Wonderful Law* (*Myōhō Renge-kyō*), which is often called *The Lotus Sutra* (*Hoke-kyō*). Similar expressions include *"Namu Butsu"* (I believe in the Buddha) and *"Namu Sambō"* (I believe in the Three Treasures).

Q: What are Mahayana sutras like?

It is thought that Mahayana sutras began to be created around the beginning of the Western era, so it cannot be said that they are the direct teachings of the Buddha. However, Mahayanist believers who sought to return to the starting point of the teachings of the Buddha reconstructed the Buddha's ideas by means of meditation, so they are surely scriptures.

Mahayanist scriptures had great subsequent ideological impact. Let us look at the most representative.

The Wisdom (Prahna) Sutras

The Japanese name for this sutra is *Han'nya-kyō*, and *hannya* is a transliteration of the Indian words *prajna* or *pannya*. The word means "wisdom," meaning the ability to know truth. It is distinguished from wisdom in the ordinary sense.

The Wisdom Sutra is not actually a single title, but is the collective name for a group of sutras which teach that enlightenment is attained via the perfection of wisdom. They include the 600-fascicle *Daihan'nya-kyo*, *Daibon-han'nya-kyō*, and the *Shōbon-han'nya-kyō*.

The Essence of Prajna-paramita Sutra, which distills the essence of *The Great Wisdom Sutra* in a mere 260-odd charac-

ピュラーなものといえます。

・法華経

『妙法蓮華経』の略称で、だれしもが仏になれることを強調しているお経です。また釈迦の入滅は方便であり、実は、この世に存在していて人々を永遠に見守っている、と説いています。

　このお経が我が国に与えた影響は計り知れません。聖徳太子、天台宗の開祖の最澄、日蓮宗を開いた日蓮などが、このお経の重要性を主張しました。

・浄土三部経

『無量寿経』『観無量寿経』『阿弥陀経』の3経をこう呼びます。極楽浄土にいる阿弥陀仏を信じ、あらゆる衆生を救済するというその偉大な力にすべてをゆだねなさいという浄土教の基本経典です。我が国では浄土宗、浄土真宗などが浄土教に該当します。

・華厳経

　釈迦の悟りの内容を示した経とされます。毘盧遮那仏という仏の光が、迷いの世界にあるすべての人々（衆生）に及び、そのため、その人々の中には仏と同じ智慧が宿っていると説いています。仏の中に衆生がおり、同時に衆生の中にも仏がいるというのです。だから衆生はだれでも悟ることができると主張しています。

ters, is probably the most popular.

The Lotus Sutra

This is the shortened name of *The Sutra of the Lotus of the Wonderful Law* and it is the sutra which stresses that anyone can become a buddha. It also preaches that the Buddha's entrance into extinction was merely an expedient and that actually he is existing in this world and eternally watching over people.

The influence this sutra has had on Japan is immeasurable. Prince Shōtoku, Saichō (founder of the Tendai Sect), and Nichiren (founder of the Nichiren Sect) all emphasized the significance of this sutra.

The Triple Pure Land Sutras

These include *The Buddha of Infinite Life Sutra* (*Muryōju-kyō*), *The Meditation on the Buddha of Infinite Life Sutra* (*Kon-muryōju-kyō*), and *The Amida Sutra* (*Amida-kyō*). These are the fundamental scriptures of Pure Land teachings which say that one should have faith in Amida Buddha who exists in the Pure Land of Utmost Bliss and entrust everything to his mighty power which can save all sentient beings. In Japan, the Pure Land Sect and the True Pure Land Sect fall within this category of Pure Land teachings.

The Garland (Kegon) Sutra

This is the sutra which is said to explicate the contents of the Buddha's enlightenment. It preaches that the light of the Buddha Vairocana shines upon all people (living beings) in the world of illusion and that because of this there dwells within those beings the same wisdom possessed by the buddhas. It says that there are sentient beings among the buddhas and buddhas among sentient beings. Therefore, the sutra stresses, any living being is capable of attaining enlightenment.

・大日経

　密教の2大聖典の1つ。『華厳経』から発展
したお経で、みずからが大宇宙としてすべてを
包み込む大日如来の偉大な慈悲心が強調されて
います。

　宇宙を構成する仏や菩薩、神々を図示したも
のを「曼荼羅」といいますが、仏の中にすべて
が含まれるという「胎蔵曼荼羅」のもとになっ
ているのがこのお経です。

・金剛頂経

　同じく密教の2大聖典の1つ。まず自分が仏
になることが強調され、今この身のままで仏に
なる「即身成仏」という考え方を生み出した
お経です。こちらは、私たち1人1人の中にす
べてが含まれているとする「金剛界曼荼羅」の
もとになりました。

Q: 仏教は、いつどこから日本に伝わってきたのですか？

　『日本書紀』は、奈良時代の政府が全力を傾け
て作った公式の歴史書です。その記述による
と、仏教が公に伝わったのは西暦に換算して
552年ということになっています。ところが、
近代の研究によると、『日本書紀』のこの部分
には政治的な混乱を隠しているような部分があ
って、史実的には疑わしいとされています。
　一方、『元興寺縁起』や『上宮聖徳法王帝
説』などという資料によると、仏教が正式にも
たらされたのは538年ということになっていま
す。こちらも確実だという証拠はないのです
が、現在は538年説のほうが有力とされている
ようです。

The Mahavairocana Sutra (Great Sun Sutra)

One of the two major scriptures of esoteric Buddhism. A development from *The Garland Sutra*, this sutra stresses the immense compassionate spirit of Dainichi Nyorai (Mahavairocana) who embodies within himself the entire universe.

Representations of the buddhas, bodhisattvas and gods that make up the universe are called *mandala*, and the Matrix-store Realm Mandala in which everything is included within the Buddha is based on this sutra.

The Diamond-Peak Sutra

The second great sutra of esoteric Buddhism. This sutra emphasizes first that one can become a buddha and it gave birth to the idea of *Sokushin jōbutsu*, becoming a buddha with one's present body. It became the basis for the Diamond Realm Mandala which portrays everything as being included within each of us.

Q: When and from where was Buddhism introduced into Japan?

The *Nihon Shoki* (*Chronicle of Japan*) is an official history to which the government of the Nara period devoted its full energies. According to this account, Buddhism was officially introduced to Japan in 552. However, according to recent research, this particular passage conceals a certain political chaos, and therefore the historicity of this account is questionable.

According to documents such as *Records of Gangōji* and *Traditions Concerning His Holiness, Prince Shōtoku*, Buddhism was officially introduced in 538. There is no definitive evidence for this date, but it is currently the most convincing theory.

いずれにしても、朝鮮半島にあった百済の聖明王が国使を遣わし、仏像や経典などを日本に送り届けたのが、日本における仏教の始まりとされています。

当時、朝鮮半島には高句麗、百済、新羅という３つの国が分立していましたが、高句麗に仏教が伝来したのが372年、百済が384年、新羅が417年といわれていますから、日本にはその１世紀半後には伝わっていたことになります。当時の東アジアの情勢から考えると、わりとスピーディーに最新の文化がもたらされたといえるのではないでしょうか。

Q: なぜ日本は仏教を受け入れたのですか？

仏教が日本に伝えられたのは538年といわれていますが、実際にはそれ以前から朝鮮半島の人々が日本に移民し、仏教を信奉していたと考えられます。その影響が日本人にも及び、ある程度、仏教が受け入れられやすい環境も整いつつあったのでしょう。

また、当時は天変地異や政治・経済的な混乱は人間の力を超えた存在のせいだと考えられていました。だから、そのような不幸を収拾し、安泰をもたらす強力な神のようなものが求められていたのです。さらに、そのころの日本は国家の黎明期で、国を支える新しい理念や倫理が必要でした。そんな日本の要請に、仏教はちょうどはまったといえると思います。

そのような状況のもと、日本では蘇我氏と物部氏という政治権力者どうしの抗争が表面化していました。両者は、仏教を日本に受け入れるかどうかということを争点にして覇を競ったと

Whichever the case, King Song of Paekche on the Korean Peninsula sent a mission to Japan bearing Buddhist images and sutras, and this is taken as the beginning of Buddhism in Japan.

At that time, there were three kingdoms on the Korean Peninsula: Koguryo, Paekche and Silla. Because it is held that Buddhism was transmitted to Koguryo in 372, Paekche in 384, and Silla in 417, this means it was another century and a half before Buddhism was transmitted to Japan. Hence, given the conditions in East Asia in those days, the wave of new culture can be said to have advanced rather rapidly.

Q: Why did Japan accept Buddhism?

It is said that Buddhism was introduced to Japan in 538, but in actual fact even before that people were leaving the Korean Peninsula to set up residence in Japan, and it is plausible that they were believers in Buddhism. Their influence may well have extended to Japanese and to some degree this may have created an environment more receptive to Buddhism.

At that time it was thought that the various natural calamities and political and economic chaos were caused by some existence that exceeded the power of human beings. Therefore, there was a desire for some powerful deity to get these misfortunes under control and bring about peace. Furthermore, that period was the dawn of Japan as a nation and new ideas and logic were needed to sustain the state. I believe one can say that Buddhism was perfectly suited to Japan's requirements.

Under these circumstances, a dispute between the politically prominent Soga and Mononobe families came to the surface. It seems that these families struggled for supremacy in Japan taking as an issue whether or not Buddhism should be

いわれています。結果は、仏教の受け入れに賛
成の蘇我氏が勝利し、仏教は日本の国土に根を
張っていくのです。

Q: 仏教はどのようにして日本に根づいていきましたか？

・飛鳥時代（6世紀末～7世紀末）

　仏教を受け入れるかどうかを巡って、賛成派
の蘇我氏と反対派の物部氏の抗争が繰り返され
ましたが、結局、賛成派の蘇我氏が勝利を収め
ました。蘇我氏は奈良に、後に飛鳥寺となる法
興寺を建て、氏寺としました。氏寺とは、寺院
であると同時に地域の権力を誇示する象徴でも
あったのです。

　ですから、これにならって各地の豪族たち
も、自分たちの力を示すためにそれぞれ氏寺を
建立しました。こうして、飛鳥仏教は氏寺を中
心にして栄えていくのです。

　そんな折、優れた政治家であった聖徳太子が
登場します。聖徳太子は用明天皇の子として生
まれましたが、おばにあたる推古天皇を補佐し
て、摂政として30年間政務を執り行います。

　聖徳太子の功績をあげればきりがありません
が、とりわけ仏教を摂取して国家の規範とし、
その普及を図ったことは重要です。具体的には
「憲法十七条」を制定し、仏・法・僧の三宝に
帰依して正義を尊び、和を強調して人心の統一
を目指したことはよく知られています。こうし
て、飛鳥時代には国家が仏教を受け入れ、その
発展の基礎を築くことになったのです。

accepted in Japan. The result was that the Soga family which favored the acceptance of Buddhism, was victorious, and Buddhism put down roots in Japanese soil.

Q: How did Buddhism establish roots in Japan?

Asuka period (late 6th century to late 7th century)

There was repeated strife between the Soga family which favored the introduction of Buddhism and the Mononobe family which opposed it, and in the end the Soga were victorious. In Nara, the Soga family built Hōkōji Temple, later to become Asukadera Temple, and made it the clan temple. At the same time that a "clan temple" was a Buddhist temple, it was also a symbol that displayed the authority of the region.

As a result, the powerful clans in other regions followed suit by constructing clan temples to exhibit their own power. In this way, Asuka Buddhism flourished around these clan temples.

At that juncture there appeared the exceptional political figure Prince Shōtoku. Born the son of Emperor Yōmei, he was appointed regent for his aunt, the Empress Suiko, and for thirty years he held the reins of administration.

There is no end to the accomplishments of Prince Shōtoku, but among them it is highly significant that he adopted Buddhism, making it the standard for the state and taking measures to diffuse it. In concrete terms, it is well known that he promulgated *The Seventeen-Article Constitution*, brought the people to devotion to the Three Treasures (the Buddha, the Buddhist law, and the community of followers), and aimed at the unification of the human mind by stressing peace. Hence, during the Asuka period the state accepted Buddhism and took Buddhism as its basis.

・奈良時代（710-794）

　8世紀、聖武天皇は奈良・平城京を都とし、強力な中央集権国家の建設を目指しました。そのために、仏教をおおいに利用したのです。聖武天皇は都に東大寺を建てて国家の象徴とし、一方で諸国に国分寺・国分尼寺を設けて中央に直結させました。国分寺・国分尼寺は地方の有力な氏族の氏寺と強く関連していましたから、中央政府が地方豪族を管理するのに、たいへん都合がよかったわけです。

奈良の大仏
Great Buddha of
Nara

　聖武天皇は、理想世界を具現する存在であり、また、天皇の権力の象徴でもある大仏の建立を命じました。そして東大寺に建てられたのが、いわゆる奈良の大仏です。同時に、諸国の国分寺・国分尼寺では、国家を守護するためのお経が盛んに唱えられました。このようにして、いやがうえでも国家意識が高められていった時代だったのです。

　このころまでに、6つの公式の仏教宗団が伝えられていました。奈良は南都と呼ばれていましたので、これらは「南都六宗」といわれます。三論宗・法相宗・華厳宗・律宗・成実宗・俱舎宗の6つです。これらは宗派というよりは、それぞれの学問のようなもので、東大寺を中心にして僧たちが学んでいたようです。

・平安時代（794-1185）

　繁栄は一方で堕落をもたらす場合もあります。奈良時代の仏教の隆盛も、教団の腐敗や、

Nara period (710-794)

In the eighth century, Emperor Shōmu made Nara and Heiankyō the capitals and sought to establish a strong centralized national authority. For that reason, Buddhism was employed to a considerable degree. Emperor Shōmu built the Todaiji and made it a symbol of the nation and in each province he built official provincial monasteries (Kokubunji) and nunneries (Kokubunniji), making them directly responsible to the center of the country. These provincial temples and nunneries were closely related to the prominent clan temples in each region, and this made it very convenient for the central government to exercise control over the regional powerful clans.

Emperor Shōmu ordered the construction of the Daibutsu (the Great Buddha) at Tōdaiji as an incarnation of the ideal world and as a symbol of the emperor's authority. This is called the Great Buddha of Nara. At the same time, at the various regional monasteries and nunneries, sutras were chanted for the protection of the nation. In this way, however averse some people might have been, it was a period when national consciousness was raised.

Up to this point, there were six formal Buddhist sects in existence. Because Nara was considered to be in the South, these sects were called the "Six Southern Sects," and they consisted of the Sanron, Hossō, Kegon, Ritsu, Jōjitsu, and Kusha. These were regarded to be different forms of scholarship rather than sects, and it seems the priests pursued their studies primarily at Tōdaiji.

Heian period (794-1185)

Prosperity sometimes brings about corruption. The prosperity of Nara-period Buddhism brought about corruption

僧侶の権力との癒着を招くことになりました。
そして仏教界は頽廃していったのです。また、
社会的にもさまざまな不安定な要因が重なり、
天変地異が打ち続くなど社会は混乱しました。

そこで桓武天皇は、人心を一新するために、
都を京都に移しました。これが平安時代の始ま
りです。そして、政府は寺院の営利事業を禁じ
るなど管理を強化し、仏教界の刷新を図りまし
た。

このような時期に登場したのが、伝教大師
最澄と弘法大師空海でした。2人とも時代の矛
盾を感じながら学問と修行に励んでいました
が、時を同じくして遣唐使船で中国に渡りまし
た。そして国を救うために、仏法を身につけて
帰国したのです。

延暦寺
Enryakuji

天台宗の法門を学んだ最澄は、その後、比叡
山に延暦寺を建て、天台法華宗を興しました。
そしてそこを仏教の総合大学とし、後に各宗の
宗祖となるような優秀な人材の育成に努めまし
た。

金剛峯寺
Kongōbuji

一方、空海は中国で密教を修め、多数の経典
や仏像、その他科学技術などを携えて帰国しま
した。そして高野山を拠点として密教を広め、
真言宗の基礎を築いたのです。空海は文化の興
隆、庶民の救済におおいに貢献しました。

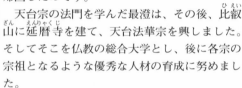

この2人の活躍によって、南都六宗の仏教と
は違う新しい平安時代の仏教が確立され、やが
て鎌倉仏教の隆盛を見ることになるのです。

within the religious orders and the monks, adherence to authority. Buddhism fell into decadence. In society as well, various
factors of unease accumulated, various natural calamities
struck one after another, and society fell into confusion.

At that point, Emperor Kanmu in an effort to renew human
nature moved the capital to Kyōto. It was the start of the Heian
Period. The government strengthened its controls, for example
in prohibiting temples from engaging in money-making activities, and attempted to reform the Buddhist world.

There then appeared Saichō, known also as Dengyō
Daishi, and Kūkai, also known as Kōbō Daishi. Both priests
continued their studies and practices despite their awareness of
the contradictions of their time, and both went to China aboard
the official diplomatic ships to the court. They devoted themselves to the Buddhist Law in an effort to save the nation.

Saichō studied the teachings of the Tendai sect, and upon
his return he established Enryakuji at Mt. Hiei and founded the
Tendai sect. It thereafter performed the role of a comprehensive Buddhist university and cultivated the kind of superior tal-
ent that would become future founders of the various sects.

Kūkai, on the other hand, practiced esoteric Buddhism in
China, and when he returned he brought back large numbers of
sutras, Buddhist figures, and types of scientific technology. He
propagated esoteric Buddhism from the focal point of Mt.
Kōya and established the foundations of Shingon Buddhism.
Kukai made great contributions to the flourishing of culture
and the salvation of the ordinary people.

As a result of the activities of these two men, a new Heian-
period Buddhism was established that was different from the
Six Southern Sects of Buddhism, and this led to the later flourishing of Kamakura Buddhism.

・鎌倉時代 (1185-1333)

　鎌倉時代は、源氏が平家を滅ぼすことからスタートしました。それに象徴されるように、この時代は戦乱が相次ぎ、また飢餓や疫病、天災が人々を襲いました。

　そのような状況を背景に次々と新興宗教が起こってきます。それらはすべて、苦難の世を克服し、苦しむ人々を救済するという共通項を持っていました。それまでは、どちらかというと国家のために機能していた仏教が、この時代になって庶民のために開かれていったのです。

　天台宗は比叡山で隆盛を極め、多くの僧兵を抱える大勢力になっていました。そして、またしても既成教団は腐敗の道を歩んでいたのです。

　鎌倉新仏教の教祖たちは、みんなそのような比叡山から巣立っていきました。堕落した教団に背を向け、山を下りて新しい仏教を目指したのです。

　まず法然がそうでした。法然は念仏さえ称えればだれでも極楽に往生できるという浄土宗を開いて、広く大衆に受け入れられました。また、その弟子の親鸞は師の教えを発展させ、浄土真宗の教義を確立しました。

　栄西や道元もまた比叡山を下りて宋に渡り、禅を学んで我が国にもたらしました。

　日蓮も比叡山を下り、日蓮宗を起こして人々を教化しましたし、一遍は時宗を立て、全国を修行のために歩きまわって阿弥陀仏の救いを説きました。

Kamakura period (1185-1333)

Kamakura period commenced with the overthrow of the Heike by the Minamoto. As if symbolized by this conflict, this era saw one disturbance after another, and the people were afflicted by famine, epidemics and natural disasters.

Against such a background, new religions sprang up one after another. Each of these religions shared in common the overcoming of the world of suffering and the salvation of people who were suffering. Until this period, Buddhism had tended to function on behalf of the nation, but in this era it expanded to espress concern for the salvation of ordinary citizens.

The Tendai Sect reached a peak of prosperity on Mt. Hiei, possessing a large group of monk-warriors. Again the established religious orders trod along the path of degeneration.

All of the founders of new Buddhist groups in Kamakura had started out in Mt. Hiei. Turning their backs on the corrupt religious orders, they descended from the mountain and aimed at a new Buddhism.

The first was Hōnen. Hōnen established the Jōdo Sect which taught that if anyone intoned the Nenbutsu he or she would be reborn in the Pure Land and brought in the broad multitude. His disciple Shinran developed his teacher's teachings even further and established the teachings of the Jōdo Shin sect.

Eisai and Dōgen also descended from Mt. Hiei, took passage to Sung China, studied Ch'an Buddhism and brought it back to Japan as Zen.

Nichiren came down from the mountain temple, formed the Nichiren sect and propagated it. Ippen founded the Ji sect and wandered across the land preaching the salvation of Amida Buddha.

　このように、現在に伝わる宗派のほとんどは鎌倉時代にスタートしたのです。その意味で、鎌倉時代は我が国の宗教改革の時代だったといえるでしょう。

・**室町時代**（1333-1568）

　鎌倉時代に起こった新仏教は、室町時代になると大きな教団に成長していきます。その理由は、仏教が民衆化したためといえます。しかし、仏教の民衆化とは必ずしも、それぞれの宗派の創始者たちの理念を深めることではありませんでした。この時代には観音信仰や地蔵信仰、七福神信仰など、ご利益を求める庶民の宗教が流行したのです。庶民が力を持ってきた時代といえます。

　政治的には荘園制が敷かれ、大きな寺は自分の荘園を持っていました。そしてそこに隷属する末寺から税を徴収できるため、経済的に安定している寺院が多かったようです。

　各宗派を概観すると、禅宗では、臨済宗が室町幕府に保護され、全盛を迎えます。曹洞宗は民衆の教化に力を入れ、おおいに信者を広げました。

　浄土真宗には蓮如が出て、比叡山の迫害にもめげずに各地を転々としながら門徒を増やし、大教団としての本願寺を築きました。この教団が政治的にも力を持ち、一向一揆を起こしたことも忘れることはできません。同様に日蓮宗も法華一揆を起こすなど、宗教のエネルギーが噴出したのもこの時代でした。

As can be seen, virtually all of the sects that have come down to the present day originated in the Kamakura period. In this sense, the Kamakura period was a period of religious reformation in Japan.

Muromachi period (1333-1568)

The new Buddhist groups that arose in the Kamakura period developed into major religious organizations in the Muromachi period. Surely the reason for this was that Buddhism had become popularized. However, the popularization of Buddhism meant that there was no deepening of the ideas of the respective sect founders. In this period belief in Kannon, Jizō and the Seven Deities of Good Fortune were popular among commoners seeking profits. It was a period when the masses came to have power.

In the political realm the estate system was expanded and large temples came to hold their own estates. Because they could collect taxes from their subordinate branch temples, many temples were able to achieve economic stability.

From an overview of the sects, we can say that the Zen school prospered greatly, with the Rinzai sect enjoying the protection of the Muromachi bakufu. The Sōto sect made great efforts to enlighten the masses and expanded its adherents considerably.

Within the Jōdo Shin sect appeared Ren'nyo, and as he sought refuge in various places to escape the persecution of Mt. Hiei monks, he increased the numbers of his followers, building Honganji into a large religious organization. This order had political clout as well, and it cannot be forgotten that it brought about the Ikkō uprising. It was an age when religious energy exploded, such as in the Hokke uprising led by the Nichiren sect.

・**安土桃山時代**（1568-1600）、**江戸時代**（1600-1868）

　戦国時代、織田信長や豊臣秀吉は、一向一揆や法華一揆を徹底して弾圧して、無力化を図りました。

　戦国時代を制した江戸幕府は、こうして弱体化した仏教を統制し、寺院を権力下に収めます。その政策として代表的なものをあげるとすれば、それは「寺檀制度」でしょう。

　この制度は、島原・天草の乱（1637年）をきっかけに、隠れキリシタンを取り締まるという名目で実施されたものでした。信仰する宗教を調べ、特定の寺の檀家であることを証明させる制度が行われたのです。檀家が所属する寺は、それぞれの家ごとの家族構成や名前などを、役所に届けました。いわば、現在の役所の戸籍係の仕事を寺が請け負っていたわけです。

　この制度によって、住民は必ずどこかの寺に所属しなければならず、また国民として幕府に管理されるようになったのです。現在、多くの家がどこかの寺の檀家となっているのは、この制度の影響が残っているからです。

　こうして、江戸時代には仏教は幕府権力の中に組み込まれていきましたが、一方では安定した庶民の信仰を得て、庶民仏教が花開いた時代でもありました。遍路や巡礼などが流行し、講という組織が組まれて集団で参拝が行われました。それによって寺社はおおいに潤ったのです。

・**明治時代**（1868-1912）

　明治維新とともに、仏教界にも大きな試練が

Azuchi-Momoyama period (1568-1600), **Edo period** (1600-1868)

In the Period of Warring States, Oda Nobunaga and Toyotomi Hideyoshi determined to suppress the Ikkō uprisings and Hokke uprisings and render the groups powerless.

The Edo bakufu which brought the Period of Warring States under control regulated this weakened Buddhism and brought the temples under its authority. Representative of such administrative policies was the Jidan-system.

This system was implemented following the Shimabara Rebellion in 1637 as a means of suppressing the "hidden Christians." It was a system for examining religious faith and causing them to give evidence that their household was a member of a specific temple. The temple to which the family belonged then submitted to the local government the composition of each household and the members' names. The temples, in effect, bore the responsibility that local government offices now have for recording residents.

As a result of this system, residents were all required to be affiliated with some temple, and they came to be controlled as citizens of the nation by the bakufu. The fact that many households support a temple is a carryover from the effects of this system.

In this manner, Buddhism was incorporated into the national government authority during the Edo period. At the same time, they achieved a stable popular religious faith and popular Buddhism blossomed. Pilgrims and pilgrimages became popular, and this came to involve religious associations which made visits to worship as a group. As a result, the temples benefitted greatly.

Meiji period (1868-1912)

With the Meiji Restoration a great ordeal beset the Bud-

押し寄せました。天皇制を復興し護持するために、明治政府が神道を国教とする政策を取ったからです。

そのために「神仏分離令」が布告され、神も仏も共に敬うという習俗が否定されたのです。その波は、廃仏毀釈の運動を呼び起こしました。寺が襲撃されたり重要な仏像が壊されたりと、仏教界は大打撃を被りました。

しかし仏教界は粘り強く政府に働きかけ、政策の転換を迫りました。同時に仏教教団の近代化を図り、維持・再建に努めたのです。

やがて政府の政策も仏教界の意向に添うようなものになりましたが、それには皮肉なことに、江戸時代の寺檀制度のなごりで、寺と檀家が強く結びついていたことが大きな力になったようです。

この時期、西洋の学問や思想が移入され、仏教も学問的に研究されるようになりました。近代仏教学が形成されたのです。それと同時に教化のあり方や思想としての仏教も問い直され、さまざまな仏教興隆運動が展開されました。

・**大正時代**（1912-1926）、**昭和時代**（1926-1989）、**平成時代**（1989- ）

大正期に入ると、情勢は一応の安定を見、文化的な成熟の時期を迎えます。いわゆる大正デモクラシーと呼ばれる時代です。

この時代は西洋の思想やキリスト教などの影響を受け、仏教も東洋思想として真価を求められました。その結果、仏教文化が一定の評価を得た時期でもあります。

dhist world. In order to restore the emperor system and maintain it, the Meiji government adopted Shinto as the state religion.

To do this, it proclaimed a decree separating Shinto and Buddhism, negating the custom of venerating gods and buddhas together. This decree set in motion an anti-Buddhist movement. Temples were attacked, valuable Buddhist figures were destroyed, and Buddhism in general suffered a severe blow.

However, the Buddhists tenaciously set to work on the government, pressing for a reversal of policy. Meanwhile the Buddhist organizations strove to modernize and endeavored to keep going as well as rebuild.

In the end, government policy fell in line with Buddhist sentiments, and ironically the vestiges of the Jidan-system of the Edo era, which strongly bound families of adherents to temples actually wound up being quite effective.

During this period, Western scholarship and ideas were imported, and Buddhism came to be researched. Modern Buddhist scholarship was formed. At the same time, methods of instruction and Buddhism as a way of thought came to be reconsidered, and a movement for Buddhist revival developed.

Taishō period (1912-1926), **Shōwa period** (1926-1989), **Heisei period** (1989-)

In the Taishō period, with the state of affairs stabilizing somewhat, there was a time of cultural maturation, known as "Taishō Democracy."

During this period, Japan came under the influence of Western ideas and Christianity, and there was a search within the depths of Buddhism as an Eastern ideology. As a result, it was also a period in which Buddhist culture attained an estab-

　その後、日本は第2次世界大戦に突入してい
きます。仏教も軍国主義の波にのみこまれ、国
家主義を宣伝し高揚させていく役を担わされた
りもします。仏教界が汚点を残した時代だった
といえるのではないでしょうか。

　戦後、日本はめざましい勢いで復興しまし
た。そのような流れの中で、既成の仏教教団も
新しい時代に合わせたもろもろの運動を模索・
展開してきました。その中から多くの新興宗教
が勃興し、新時代を築くエネルギーとなったこ
とは記憶されるべきでしょう。

　やがてベルリンの壁が崩壊し、東西の世界対
立が氷解した今、新たな意味で宗教が求められ
ています。古い世界観が崩壊し、新しい価値観
が必要とされているのです。片方では民族主義
の波が高まり、世界の各地で宗教戦争が勃発し
ています。一方では国家という垣根を越えた地
球市民としての連体が叫ばれ、異なった宗教の
間の交流が求められています。このような事態
をどう受け止め、対処していくかが問われてい
るのが、現在の宗教状況といえるのではないで
しょうか。

lished reputation.

Following this, Japan plunged into World War II. Buddhists were also swept up in the wave of national militarism, adopting the role of promoting and exalting nationalism. This period is undoubtedly one of disgrace for Buddhists.

After the war, Japan recovered with amazing speed. Within the flow of the times, established Buddhist groups struggled and developed as they dealt with the various movements of the new age. It ought not be forgotten that in the midst of the turmoil, many new religions suddenly rose to prominence, providing the driving force for establishing a new order.

Today, with the collapse of the Berlin Wall and the easing of East-West tensions, people are seeking religion with a new purpose. The old world view has fallen apart and new values are needed. On the one hand, the tide of ethnicity has risen and around the world religious conflict has broken out. On the other hand, there are calls to go beyond national boundaries in the name of unity as world citizens, and there is a need for exchange among the different religions. It can surely be said that the current state of affairs within religion requires determining what to make of such a situation and how to deal with the changes.

日本の仏教を作った人たち

The Makers of
Japanese Buddhism

Q: 空海（774-835）はどんな人でしたか？

空海
Kūkai

真言宗の開祖です。今の四国の香川県の屏風ケ浦というところで生まれました。時は平安時代、最澄（767-822）の7つ下です。幼いころから勉強が好きだったと言われています。

都に上って、儒教や道教、仏教などを学びましたが、最終的には仏教がもっとも優れているとして仏教を選びました。彼は自分の学問の過程を、24歳の時に書いた『三教指帰』に記しています。

やがて出家して僧となり、遣唐使船に乗って

Q: What kind of person was Kūkai (774-835)?

Kūkai was the founder of Shingon or Esoteric Buddhism. He was born in Byōbugaura in present-day Kagawa prefecture in Shikoku during the Heian period, seven years after the birth of Saichō (767-822). It is said from an early age he was fond of studying.

He went to Kyōto where he studied Confucian, Taoist and Buddhist teachings, and ultimately took up the study of Buddhism after deciding it was superior. He recorded the process of his own scholarship at the age of 24 in a work titled *Indications of the Goals of the Three Teachings*.

Before long, he entered the priesthood and traveled to

中国に留学しました。この時、空海も4隻の船団の第1の船に乗っていましたが、たまたま最澄もこの船団の2番目の船に乗っていたというから奇遇です。しかし、彼らの目的は別で、空海は密教を学ぶために3年、最澄は主に天台の教学を学ぶために1年間留学しました。

空海は青竜寺の恵果のもとで勉学に励み、秀でた能力を発揮して密教の奥義を授かりました。そして多数の経典や密教の図像などを携え、帰国したのです。密教は天皇や貴族たちに受け入れられ、空海の名声はたちどころに広まりました。

彼は多くの人々に密教を伝える一方、高野山に金剛峯寺を開創して真言宗の拠点としました。また東寺を賜り、専修の道場として真言密教の基礎を確立したのです。

空海は真言宗を開くとともに日本に密教芸術を伝え、多くの著書も残して文化発展に寄与しました。そして同時に、庶民の学校である「綜芸種智院」を開くなどして民衆の教化にあたったことも忘れてはなりません。入滅後、醍醐天皇（885-930）から弘法大師という号を賜りました。

Q: 最澄（767-822）はどんな人でしたか？

天台宗の開祖です。今の滋賀県に生まれ、20歳の時に東大寺で正式に僧になりました。ところが彼は都の仏教に満足できず、比叡山にこも

T'ang China to study. He traveled on board one of the four ships of the official mission to the Chinese capital. By a strange coincidence, he was aboard the first ship in the fleet and Saichō was aboard the second ship. However, their respective goals were different, and while Kūkai studied Esoteric Buddhism for three years, Saichō studied primarily T'ien-t'ai teachings for one year.

Kūkai diligently studied under Hui-kuo at the Ching-lung Temple, where he exhibited exceptional ability and was permitted to receive the ultimate teachings of Esoteric Buddhism. He eventually returned to Japan carrying large numbers of sutras and Esoteric Buddhist images, among other things. Esoteric Buddhism was accepted by the Emperor and Kūkai rapidly became eminent.

While he transmitted Esoteric Buddhism to large numbers of people, he established Kongōbu-ji on Mt. Kōya as the center of the Shingon sect. He was then entrusted with Tōji, and established there a foundation for the practice of Shingon teachings.

Kūkai founded Esoteric Buddhism in Japan, but he also introduced Esoteric culture, contributing to the development of culture through large numbers of writings. We ought not forget that it was also Kūkai who propagated among the masses for instance by opening a school for the general public known as Shugei Shuchi-in, a school of arts and sciences. Following his death, the Emperor Daigo (885-930) bestowed upon him the posthumous title Kōbō Daishi.

Q: What kind of person was Saichō (767-822)?

Saichō was the founder of the Tendai sect. Born in present-day Shiga prefecture, he became ordained at Tōdaiji at the age of twenty. Dissatisfied with Buddhism in the capital city,

最澄
Saichō

ってしまいました。そこで、鑑真（688-763）の
もたらした中国の天台宗の祖師智顗（538-597）
の著作の勉強にいそしんだのです。

そんな最澄のうわさは天皇の耳に達し、彼は
僧として高い位を与えられました。そして、山
上に人を集め、『法華経』の講義をさせられた
のです。

そのようなことがさらに評判を呼び、最澄は
今度は中国への留学を命じられました。そし
て、空海と同じ遣唐使船の船団で唐に渡ったの
です。

最澄は天台山で天台の教学と戒律を修め、竜
興寺では密教を学び、さらに禅林寺で禅を勉強
しました。そして、多くの経典を持って帰国し
たのです。

帰国後、最澄は比叡山に一乗止観院を建てて
天台法華宗を起こし、後進の育成に当たりま
す。そこは後に、延暦寺という仏教の総合大学
になりました。

最澄の功績として、奈良仏教と論争して天台
宗の地位を高めたことと、僧になるための手続
きとして、従来行われていたものより簡単な
「大乗戒の授戒」という方法を提唱して、仏教
の隆盛を図ったことがあげられます。なお、最澄
は入滅後、伝教大師という号を与えられました。

Q: 法然（1133-1212）はどんな人でしたか？

浄土宗の開祖です。法然は1133年に今の岡山
県に生まれました。父は役人でしたが、法然が
9歳の時、敵対する人に襲われて死んでしまい
ます。それがきっかけで、法然は菩提寺で出家
したのです。

he sequestered himself on Mt. Hiei, where he diligently studied the writings of Chih-i (538-597), founder of Chinese T'ien-tai, which Ganjin (688-763) had brought back from China.

Word of Saichō reached the ears of the Emperor and Saichō was granted an elevated position. People gathered on the mountain to hear him lecture on the Lotus Sutra.

His reputation spread further and next he was appointed to study in China. Along with Kūkai, he set sail for China aboard one of the official diplomatic ships.

On Mt. T'ien-t'ai Saichō studied the doctrine and precepts of T'ien-t'ai, Esoteric Buddhism at Ryūkōji, and Ch'an at Zen-rinji. Then returned to Japan with many scriptures.

When he returned to Japan, Saichō built on Mt. Hiei the Ichijōshikan'in, established the Tendai sect and spent the rest of his life cultivating the teachings. This was later to become the comprehensive school of Buddhist studies known as Enryakuji.

Among his meritorious accomplishments are Saichō's elevation of the Tendai sect by means of debates with Nara Buddhists and, by his advocacy of a simpler method of ordination than had previously been allowed, his efforts to make Buddhism more prosperous. After he died, he was bestowed the posthumous title Dengyō Daishi.

Q: What kind of person was Hōnen (1133-1212)?

Hōnen was the founder of the Jōdo (Pure Land) sect. He was born in 1133 in present-day Okayama prefecture. His father was an official and was killed in a fight when Hōnen was nine. After that, Hōnen left his family to live in the care of the family temple.

法然
Hōnen

　その後、法然は比叡山に上り、天台の教学
や、その他多くの仏教の教理を学びましたが、
納得のいく理解を得ることができませんでし
た。

　ところがある時、法然は1冊の書物を読んで
いて目をくぎづけにされてしまいました。それ
は中国の浄土教の大成者、善導（613-681）の書
いた『観無量寿経疏』という書物でした。そ
こには、「自分は悟る力などない凡夫であるこ
とを自覚し、ひたすら阿弥陀仏にすがりなさ
い。阿弥陀仏はそういう人を救ってくれるの
だ」と書いてありました。法然はこれを読ん
で、自力で悟ろうとするうぬぼれが、むしろ解
脱をはばんでいるのだということを知ったので
す。

　法然は比叡山を下り、念仏だけ称えればだれ
でも平等に極楽浄土へ往生できる、という専修
念仏を人々に説きました。その教えは、自力の
修行など不可能な一般大衆に広く支持されたの
です。

　この専修念仏が庶民の間に爆発的な広がりを
みせると、旧来の南都や比叡山の僧たちは危機
感を抱き、政府を動かして弾圧をかけてきまし
た。そして、ついに法然は四国に流罪になって
しまいます。しかし、そのことは逆に、法然に
対する人々の信仰を強めたといえます。法然は
翌年には流罪を解かれ、数年後、京都の東山大
谷に住んで、教化を続けました。そして、その
地で80歳の生涯を閉じたのです。

Later Hōnen was sent to Mt. Hiei where he studied Tendai doctrines as well as doctrines of other forms of Buddhism, but he remained unconvinced and dissatisfied.

One day when he was reading the *Commentary on the Meditation Sutra* by Chinese Pure Land master Shan-tao (613-681), his eyes came to a striking passage. It said that one should awaken to the fact that one is an ordinary being without the ability to achieve enlightenment, and that one need only rely upon Amida Buddha. When Hōnen read this, he recognized that his conceit in attempting to attain enlightenment by his own strength was actually impeding his emancipation.

Hōnen then left Mt. Hiei and began preaching to the people "the exclusive practice of the *nembutsu*," which means that if one but practices invocation of the name of the Buddha one will unfailingly attain rebirth in the Pure Land. That teaching received wide support from the general populace for whom practices dependent on their own strength were formerly impossible.

When this exclusive practice of the *nembutsu* spread rapidly among the commoners, the priests of the older Nara schools and those of Mt. Hiei sensed a crisis coming on. They sought the government's help in suppressing the movement. Eventually Hōnen was even banished to Shikoku. However, this had the reverse effect of strengthening the people's belief in Hōnen. The following year the banishment was lifted, and for several years thereafter Hōnen took residence in Ōtani in Higashiyama and continued to spread his ideas. He died there at the age of eighty.

Q: 親鸞 (1173-1262) はどんな人でしたか?

法然の弟子で、師の教えを発展させて、浄土真宗を開いた人です。

親鸞
Shinran

彼は1173年、京都の公家の家に生まれました。しかし、公家とは名ばかりの貧しさで、9歳の時に出家させられます。彼はその後、比叡山に上り、あるお堂の堂僧を務めました。

親鸞は、自分の欲望や執着を正面から見つめ、真剣に悩む性格だったようです。そのような親鸞の悩みを、比叡山の僧や教理は救ってはくれませんでした。そんな折、よく彼の耳に入ってくるのは巷で布教する法然のうわさでした。

解決できない苦悩を抱えた親鸞は、聖徳太子が創建した六角堂に、100ヵ日参籠することに決めました。そして95日目、親鸞の夢に観音菩薩が現れて、彼の煩悩を肯定する言葉を告げたのです。

堂を出た親鸞は、煩悩を持ったまま阿弥陀仏を信ぜよ、と説く法然のもとを訪ねました。その出会いが親鸞の運命を変えたのです。彼は法然の教えを聞いて感動し、即座に弟子入りしました。

法然のもとで浄土宗の奥義を究めた親鸞でしたが、法然が四国に流罪になる時、連座して今の新潟県に流されてしまいました。35歳の時です。

4年後に赦免になると、親鸞は今の茨城県に行き、念仏の教えを説き広めます。阿弥陀仏にすべてを委ねればいいという絶対他力の教えは、この地の人々の心をとらえました。主著の『教行信証』もこの地で書かれたといいます。

Q: What kind of person was Shinran (1173-1262)?

A disciple of Hōnen, Shinran developed his teacher's ideas and founded the Jōdo Shin sect of Pure Land Buddhism.

He was born in a family of the nobility in 1173. But his family was poor and noble in name only, so when he was nine, he was sent to live in a temple. Later he was sent to serve as a menial monk at one of the temples on Mt. Hiei.

It appears that Shinran's personality led him to stare straight at and be seriously distressed by his own desires and attachments. Neither the monks nor the doctrines on Mt. Hiei were able to save Shinran from this anguish. It was then that he heard regular rumors about Hōnen propagating in the city.

Bearing this unresolvable anguish, Shinran decided to carry out a hundred-day retreat at Rokkaku-dō, which had been constructed by Prince Shōtoku. On the ninety-fifth day, Kannon Bosatsu appeared in Shinran's dream and proclaimed an affirmation of his sufferings.

Shinran left the hall, his anguish intact, and visited Hōnen who was preaching his belief in Amida Buddha. This encounter changed Shinran's life. Upon hearing Hōnen's teachings, he was deeply moved and he immediately became a follower.

As Hōnen's disciple, Shinran was able to delve into the depths of the teachings of the Jōdo sect, but when Hōnen was banished to Shikoku, Shinran too was implicated and sent to what is now Niigata prefecture. He was then thirty-five.

Pardoned four years later, Shinran set out for present-day Ibaraki prefecture where he spread the teachings of the *nembutsu*. The preaching of the absolute power of the other, that one need only trust entirely in Amida Buddha, captured the hearts of the people in that region. It is also said that it was there that he wrote *Teaching, Practice, Faith, Attainment*.

　　　　しばらく関東地方で布教を続けた後、親鸞は
京都に居を移し、多くの著作を残しました。そ
して90歳でこの世を去ったのです。

Q: 日蓮（にちれん）（1222-1282）はどんな人でしたか？

日蓮
Nichiren

　　　　日蓮宗の開祖です。1222年、日蓮は今の千葉
県の安房小湊（あわこみなと）の網元の家に生まれましたが、少
年の時に地元の清澄寺（せいちょうじ）で僧となりました。その
後、彼は京に上り、比叡山で勉学にいそしみま
した。

　　　　11年後、日蓮は再び清澄寺に帰りました。そ
してそれまでの体験から『法華経（ほけきょう）』のみが真実
の教えであることを確信し、『法華経』を広め
ることを決意して、日蓮宗を起こすことを宣言
したのです。

　　　　日蓮の思想は、法華経信仰以外の仏教をこと
ごとく否定する過激なものでした。そのため彼
は故郷を追われ、鎌倉で布教活動を行いまし
た。

　　　　当時、天災飢饉が猛威をふるって人々を苦し
めていました。日蓮は国が『法華経』を信奉し
ないせいだとして『立正安国論（りっしょうあんこくろん）』を著し、幕
府に提示しました。ところがこれが幕府の怒り
を買うことになり、日蓮は伊豆に流されてしま
ったのです。

　　　　翌年には赦免になりましたが、その後、蒙古（もうこ）
のフビライ・ハーンから幕府に屈伏を促す手紙
が届き、日蓮は『立正安国論』の正しさを確信
しました。そこで彼はさらに各所で自説を主張（げきりん）
しました。しかし、これがまた幕府の逆鱗に触
れ、今度は彼は打ち首を命じられます。だが罪
一等を減ぜられ、佐渡（さど）に流されました。

After continuing propagation in the Kantō area for a while, Shinran moved to Kyōto where he wrote a large number of works. He left this world at the age of ninety.

Q: What kind of person was Nichiren (1222-1282)?

Nichiren was the founder of the Nichiren sect. He was born into the family of a fisherman in 1222 in Kominato, Awa Province, in what is now Chiba prefecture. While still a boy he determined to become a priest at Seichōji near his home. He later decided to go to Kyōto and to study at Mt. Hiei.

Eleven years later he returned to Seichōji, having become convinced from all his experiences to that point that he believed that the Lotus Sutra was the only true teaching. Determined to expound the *Lotus Sutra*, he declared his intention of establishing the Nichiren sect.

Nichiren's thought was a radical denial of all Buddhism with the exception of the *Lotus Sutra*. For this reason he was forced out of his home province and carried out his propagating activities in Kamakura.

At that time a series of natural disasters, famine and epidemics plagued the populace. Nichiren set out his conviction that these calamities were the result of not embracing the *Lotus Sutra* in his *Treatise on the Establishment of the True Dharma and the Peace of the Nation* and submitted it to the government. This earned him the antipathy of the military government and he was banished to Izu.

He received a pardon, and later, when an envoy delivered to the government a letter from the Mongolian leader Khubilai Khan demanding tribute, he took this as evidence of the accuracy of his treatise. He traveled from place to place proclaiming his own views. This further raised the shackles of the government and this time he was sentenced to beheading. He received a reprieve, however, and was only banished to Sado

　赦免後、日蓮は再び幕府に『法華経』信仰を
進言しましたが聞き入れてもらえず、今の山梨
県の身延山（みのぶさん）に隠棲して、弟子たちの育成にあた
りました。

　1282年、療養のために身延を下り、今の東京
都大田区にある池上（いけがみ）という在家信者の家に立ち
寄ったところで、日蓮はその生涯を終えたので
す。

Q: 一遍（いっぺん）（1239－1289）はどんな人でしたか？

　時宗（じしゅう）の開祖です。時宗は浄土教の一派で、藤
沢の遊行寺（ゆぎょうじ）（清浄光寺）が本山です。

　一遍は今の愛媛県に生まれました。幼くして
法然の孫弟子に師事しましたが、一度僧をやめ
て俗界に戻りました。しかし、その後再び志を
立てて出家し、長野県の善光寺（ぜんこうじ）を詣でた後、今
の愛媛県にある寺にこもって激しい修行をしま
した。そして、そこで阿弥陀仏と一体になる宗
教体験をしたのです。

　一遍は、心にほんとうの信心があるかどうか
は別にして、一度でも口にまかせて「南無阿弥
陀仏」と称えれば、極楽に往生できると確信し
ました。そして、それを人々に説くことを決心
したのです。

　その後一遍は、自分に帰依（きえ）した尼僧3人とと
もに全国各地を遊行します。その折、「南無阿
弥陀仏決定往生六十万人（けつじょうおうじょう）」と書かれた札を
人々に配り、1人でも多くの人に念仏との縁を
結んでもらうようにしました。

Island.

Nichiren was pardoned, and once again he submitted a memorial to the government promoting faith in the *Lotus Sutra*, which also went unheeded. He retired to a secluded place on Mt. Minobu in present-day Yamanashi prefecture, cultivating his following.

In 1282 he descended from Mt. Minobu for medical care and at the home of a lay follower named Ikegami, in what is now Ōta ward in Tōkyō, Nichiren left this world.

Q: What kind of person was Ippen (1239-1289)?

Ippen was the founder of the Ji sect, a branch of the Jōdo school, which has its main temple Yugyōji (Shōjōkōji) in Fuji-sawa.

Born in present-day Ehime prefecture, Ippen at an early age studied under a disciple of Hōnen. He left the priesthood once and returned to the secular world. However, he once again resolved to enter the priesthood, and after a pilgrimage to Zenkōji in Nagano prefecture, he went to a secluded temple in Ehime prefecture where he carried out rigorous religious prac-tices. It was there that he had his religious experience of becoming one with Amida Buddha.

Ippen was convinced that whether or not one was truly devout at heart, if a person even once intoned "Namu Amida Butsu," he or she would be reborn in the Pure Land. He deter-mined that he would preach this message.

Thereafter he, along with three devoted followers, wan-dered throughout the entire country. They constantly handed out slips of paper saying, "Take refuge in Amida Buddha; defi-nite rebirth; six hundred thousand believers," in an attempt to bring even one more person into the fold of *nembutsu* practi-

　一遍の説法は熱を帯び、聴衆は恍惚とし、踊り出したといいます。彼はそのようにして、大勢の人々を教化したのです。

　一遍は51歳の時に亡くなりました。生涯、財物を持つことを自分に禁じた彼は、亡くなる時に自分の著書をすべて焼き尽くさせたといいます。そのため、彼の著書はいっさい残っていません。

Q: 栄西（えいさい）（1141-1215）はどんな人でしたか？

栄西
Eisai

　禅宗の1つである臨済宗（りんざいしゅう）の開祖です。彼は神社に生まれたのですが、子供の時に出家しました。

　栄西は後に比叡山に上って仏教を学びました。しかし、権力争いにうつつを抜かす僧たちの堕落ぶりに愛想をつかし、また中国で禅が栄えていることを聞いて山を下り、宋に渡りました。

　栄西は阿育王山（あいくおうざん）などで仏教を学びましたが、中国での禅の隆盛に驚かされます。心身をさわやかにする茶道の存在を知ったのもこの時で、お茶を最初に日本にもたらしたのは栄西だったのです。

　およそ半年後に帰国した栄西は、比叡山に中国から持ちかえった多くの書物を献上しました。しかし、彼は比叡山にはとどまらず、九州に渡って布教活動を行います。

　47歳の時、栄西は再び中国に渡りました。宋を経由してインドに行こうとしたのです。しかし、この試みは官憲に妨害されて失敗に終わりました。

　この留学の時、栄西は虚庵懐敞（こあんえしょう）と出会い、師

tioners.

It is said that those who heard him preach became excited and started to dance enraptured. In this way, he converted large numbers of people.

Ippen died at age fifty-one. Having denied himself possessions throughout his life, he is said to have had all of his writings burned upon his death. As a result, not one of his writings remains today.

Q: What kind of person was Eisai (1141-1215)?

Eisai was the founder of the Rinzai sect of Zen Buddhism. He was born into a family affiliated with a shrine, but began to study Buddhism at an early age.

Eisai later went to study at Mt. Hiei. However, he became disillusioned with the constant conflicts over authority and the depravity of the priests, so upon hearing that Ch'an teachings were flourishing in China, he left Hiei and took passage to China.

Eisai studied Buddhism at such places as Mount A-yu-wang and was astounded by the prosperity of Ch'an in China. This was also when it became known that tea had a soothing effect on mind and body, and it was Eisai who first introduced tea to Japan.

About half a year later, Eisai returned to Japan and presented a large number of scriptures from China to the temple at Mt. Hiei. However, he did not return to Mt. Hiei to live, and instead crossed over to Kyūshū to spread the teachings.

At the age of forty-seven, Eisai again went to Sung China. He attempted to travel through China to India, but was thwarted by authorities.

During his time abroad, Eisai met Hsu-an Huai-ch'ang,

事しました。虚庵は臨済宗黄竜派の禅の名僧です。

　4年後に師から禅の極意を会得したことを認められ、栄西は帰国しました。そして九州で布教活動を再開しますが、比叡山の僧たちのねたみを受けて弾圧されました。

　そこで栄西は、鎌倉に居を移しました。当時発足したばかりの鎌倉幕府は、京都に対抗して新しい文化や宗教を必要としていました。栄西の禅はそのような新天地の要望と合致し、将軍家の帰依を受けて臨済宗を広めたのです。

　その後、栄西は京都に戻り、75歳で入滅しました。

Q: 道元（1200-1253）はどんな人でしたか？

道元
Dōgen

　禅の一宗である曹洞宗の開祖です。道元は貴族の家に生まれましたが、幼くして両親を失ってしまいました。そして13歳の時、比叡山で出家しました。ところが当時の比叡山では僧兵が幅をきかせ、仏教は本来の純粋性をなくしていました。道元はそんな状況にがまんがならず、わずか2年ほどで山を下りてしまいました。そして建仁寺に栄西を訪ね、禅を知ったのです。

　栄西が亡くなった後、道元は中国に渡りました。そして自分を真の仏道に導いてくれる師を求め、諸寺を巡り歩きました。やがて天童山を訪ねた時、優れた禅僧如浄と出会ったのです。

　如浄のもとで必死で修行に励んだ道元は、ある日ふと不思議な体験をしました。自分の心の中から自我が消え去ったように感じたのです。これが道元の悟りの体験でした。

master of the Huang-lung school of Lin-chi Ch'an (Rinzai Zen) and became his student.

Four years later his teacher gave recognition that Eisai had attained the ultimate understanding of Zen, and Eisai returned to Japan. He renewed mission activities in Kyūshū but due to the jealousy of Mt. Hiei priests his activities were prohibited by the court.

Eisai then moved to Kamakura. The newly founded Kamakura shogunate was seeking new elements of culture and religion to strengthen itself against the Kyōto court. Eisai's Zen corresponded with the needs of this new realm, and with the patronage of the shogunate, the Rinzai sect grew.

Later returning to Kyōto, Eisai entered nirvana at the age of seventy-five.

Q: What kind of person was Dōgen (1200-1253)?

Dōgen was the founder of the Sōtō school of Zen. He was born into a family of the nobility, but when he was still a child he lost both of his parents. At the age of thirteen, he went to Mt. Hiei determined to become a priest. At that time, however, Mt. Hiei was a place where warrior-monks sought influence and where Buddhism had lost its original purity. Unable to endure the situation, Dōgen left the temple within two years. He went to Kenninji, visited Eisai and learned about Zen.

After Eisai's death, Dōgen crossed over to China. Seeking a teacher who would guide him to the true path of Buddhism, Eisai visited various temples. Finally he came to Mt. T'ien-t'ung where he met the exceptional Ch'an priest Ju-ching.

One day as he was earnestly and devotedly practicing under the guidance of Ju-ching, Dōgen had an amazing experience. He felt as if his "self" had disappeared from within his own mind. This was Dōgen's experience of spiritual awakening.

　4年間の留学を終えて、道元は帰国しました。そして建仁寺を経て山城の深草に居住し、数々の著作を残しました。そんな道元に帰依する人は、日を追って増えていきました。

　旧仏教勢力はこれをねたみ、圧力を加えてきました。道元はこのような政治的動向との接触を嫌い、今の福井県の志比庄に居を移しました。そして大仏寺を開創して弟子の指導にあたったのです。これが後の永平寺です。

　道元はその後、一時、将軍に呼ばれて鎌倉に行ったりしますが、すぐに福井に帰って世俗とは一線を画して禅の高揚に努め、54歳で亡くなりました。

After four years of studying abroad, Dōgen returned home. Residing first at Kenninji, he later moved to a temple in Fukakusa where he wrote numerous works. The number of people who venerated Dōgen increased day by day.

He drew the enmity of older Buddhist forces and they put pressure on him. Disliking having to contend with such political movements, Dōgen moved to Shihinoshō in present-day Fukui prefecture. There he founded Daibutsuji and devoted his energies to the training of his disciples. This is the temple that was later renamed Eiheiji.

Dōgen was invited by the Shōgun to come to Kamakura, but he soon returned to Fukui, determined to elevate Zen by separating it from the world of secular affairs. He entered nirvana at the age of fifty-four.

仏教の宗派の特徴

Features of the Sects of
Buddhism

Q: 華厳宗とはどんな宗派ですか？

　　奈良時代，南都（奈良）には6つの宗派があって南都六宗と呼ばれていました。しかし、実際には宗派というより学派のようなもので、僧たちは各学派の教理を研究していたようです。

　　その南都六宗の1つが華厳宗で、『華厳経』（80ページ参照）の教えをよりどころとしています。『華厳経』には毘盧遮那仏という仏が登場します。毘盧遮那仏とは「ヴァイローチャナ」という古代インドの言葉を音写したもので、「あまねく照らす」という意味です。すな

5

Q: What is the Kegon sect?

During the Nara period, there were six sects of Buddhism in the Southern capital, Nara, which came to be called "the Six Sects of Nara Buddhism." In actuality they were schools more than sects, and it seems that priests studied the doctrines of each of the schools.

One of the six was the Kegon (Flower Garland) school, which laid stress on the *Sutra of the Garland Buddhas* (see page 81) in which appears the *Birushana Butsu*, a transliteration of the Indian word Vairocana, which means "forever shining." In other words, Buddhist spiritual wisdom is compared to the light of the sun.

わち、仏の智慧を太陽の光にたとえているのです。

ところで、奈良・東大寺にある奈良の大仏は、この毘盧遮那仏です。聖武天皇が３年の歳月をかけて作らせた国家の象徴ともいうべき寺と仏像ですが、この東大寺が華厳宗の大本山です。

華厳宗の宗祖は良弁といわれています。良弁は法相宗の学者でしたが、聖武天皇に請われて金鐘寺の住職となり、新羅から審祥を招いて『華厳経』の講義を受けました。これが我が国初の『華厳経』の公開だったようです。それで後に東大寺が作られた折、良弁が入寺して華厳宗の宗祖（または第二祖）といわれるようになったのでしょう。

その後も脈々と法統は受け継がれてきましたが、宗団としての規模は小さく、末寺は約40ほどです。

Q: 法相宗とはどんな宗派ですか？

南都六宗の１つです。私たちのものを見る目は幻想に惑わされています。きれいだとか汚いとか、豊かだとか貧しいとか、そんな世間の価値のレベルでレッテルが貼りつけられているからです。そのような表面に現れている現象を「相」といいます。そして、幻想を取り払った真実の姿を「法の性」といいます。その法の性と相を見極めようというねらいがあるので、「法相宗」と呼ばれるのです。

この宗は、別名を「唯識宗」ともいいます。あらゆる事物は、私たちの認識によって存在するのであり、心の認識のみがあって、心のほかにはなにも存在しないと考えるからです。

The Great Buddha of the Tōdaiji in Nara is this Vairocana Buddha. Built by the Emperor Shōmu over a period of three years as a temple and statue to symbolize the nation, Tōdaiji is the main object of worship of the Kegon sect.

The founder of the Kegon sect is said to have been Rōben, a scholar of the Hossō school who at the request of Emperor Shōmu became head priest of Konshu-ji and who invited the Korean priest Shen-hsiang (Shinjō) to deliver lectures on the *Kegon Sutra*. It appears that this was the first introduction of the *Kegon Sutra* in Japan. Later when the Tōdaiji was completed, Rōben entered the temple and became the founder (some say the second patriarch) of the Kegon sect.

This tradition has remained to the present, but the sect remains small, with approximately forty associated temples.

Q: What is the Hossō sect?

The Hossō school is one of the six schools of Nara Buddhism. According to it, what we see is distorted by illusion. We think things are pretty or dirty, luxurious or miserable depending upon the labels placed on them by the values of society. The phenomena which appear on the surface are called "aspects." True form with all illusions removed is referred to as the "real nature of the Law." Because it aims at distinguishing between real nature and mere superficial aspects, it came to be called the Hossō sect.

It is also known as the Consciousness-Only sect. This is because it holds that we determine the existence of all things in the consciousness. Because all things exist within our consciousness, it holds further that nothing exists outside of our mind.

そして、私たちの具体的な認識の機能として、五感とそれを統合する意識をあげ、そのほかにマナ識とアーラヤ識という深層心理があって、私たちの認識を左右していると説きます。そのアーラヤ識を浄化することによって悟りが得られると考えるのです。

『西遊記』のモデルにもなった唐の玄奘三蔵がインドに渡ってこの思想に傾倒し、その注釈書を中国に持ち帰りました。そして慈恩大師窺基の助力を得て訳したのが『成唯識論』10巻で、これが法相宗の聖典になっているのです。

興福寺
Kōfukuji

以上のような経過から、法相宗では玄奘三蔵を始祖とし、慈恩大師を宗祖としています。日本には唐の時代から道昭（629-700）などによって数度にわたって伝えられ、元興寺、興福寺を中心に広められました。

日本ではもっとも古く、同時にもっとも小さな宗派でもあります。興福寺と薬師寺を大本山とし、昭和25年に聖徳宗を立てるまでは法隆寺も大本山でした。

Q:律宗とはどんな宗派ですか？

南都六宗の1つ。仏教の僧になるには、戒律を授かり、それを守る約束をすることが必要です。それを「授戒」といいます。ところが、当時、日本には正式に戒律を伝える資格を持った僧がいませんでした。そこで日本の僧が中国に派遣され、唐の名僧鑑真和上に来朝を願いました。

鑑真はこれを承諾しましたが、政府が許可を

Our actual consciousness functions by means of the five sense organs and the consciousness that unifies them. In addition there is a deep psychology of mana-consciousness and alaya-consciousness which causes our consciousness to move this way and that. By purifying this alaya-consciousness we can achieve awakening.

Hsuan-tsang of the T'ang era, who became the model for *The Journey to the West* traveled to India where he devoted himself to the study of Indian thought, returning to China bringing commentaries on those texts. With the help of K'uei-chi (Jion Daishi) he translated the ten-volume *Treatise on the Establishment of the Doctrine of Consciousness Only* (Jōyuishikiron), which is the basic scripture of the Hosso sect.

Hence Hsuang-tsang is considered the founder and K'uei-chi is considered the first patriarch of the Hossō sect. The teachings were transmitted to Japan several times within the T'ang period by such people as Dōshō (629-700), where they were centered on Gangōji and Kōfukuji.

It is the oldest and also the smallest sect in Japan. The main temples are Kōfukuji and Yakushiji, as was Hōryūji until the Shōtoku sect made that its main temple in 1950.

Q: What is the Ritsu sect?

The Ritsu sect is one of the six schools of Nara Buddhism. In order to become a Buddhist priest one has to accept the precepts and promise to obey them. This was called "receiving the precepts." However, at the time there was no priest in Japan who possessed the credentials for formally transmitting the precepts. Therefore, Japanese priests were sent to China to request that the eminent priest Ganjin (Chien-chen) come to Japan.

Ganjin accepted the invitation, but the Chinese govern-

鑑真
Ganjin

唐招提寺
Tōshōdaiji

出しません。そこで鑑真らは密出国を計って日本に渡ろうとしましたが、風雨などに遭って何度も失敗しました。鑑真はそのため失明してしまいますが、それでもくじけず、11年目、5回目のトライでついに日本にやって来ます。

　日本に来た鑑真は奈良に唐招提寺を開き、ここに日本の律宗がスタートしたのです。

　ところで、戒律と一言でいいますが、戒と律とはもともと別のものです。戒は在家信者の守るべき規範で、律は教団の規則です。だから前者には罰則規定がありませんが、後者にはあるのです。

　ところが、仏教が中国に入ると、そのへんが混同されてしまいます。戒と律は、戒律という言葉で一括りにされてしまったのです。それを中国で初めて整理・体系化したのが初唐の高僧南山律師道宣で、鑑真は道宣の孫弟子にあたります。

　鎌倉時代、律宗は唐招提寺、戒壇院西大寺、泉涌寺に派が分かれ、各寺が本山と称しました。ところが明治政府の仏教政策で、律宗は真言宗に包括されてしまいました。そのため、現在はこれに抵抗した唐招提寺のみが律宗を名乗っています。

Q: 真言宗とはどんな宗派ですか？

　弘法大師空海が中国から、仏像、経典を持ってきて日本に確立させた宗派です。本山は空海が創建した高野山金剛峯寺ですが、その後さまざまに派が分かれ、多くの派と本山があります。

ment would not give its permission. Ganjin and the priests then planned to sneak him out of the country illegally, but they failed repeatedly to cross to Japan due to storms and other mishaps. In one accident he even lost his eyesight, but he still did not surrender, and eleven years later on his fifth attempt he finally succeeded in reaching Japan.

Upon arriving in Japan, Ganjin established Tōshōdaiji and this is where the Ritsu sect began in Japan.

We speak of "precepts" as one thing, but actually they comprise two categories of rules which lay believers are required to follow and regulations for the religious orders. There are no punitive provisions in the former, but there are in the latter.

When Buddhism entered China, these two categories became merged. "Precepts" and "regulations" became subsumed under the all-inclusive "precepts." The first to organize and compile these was an eminent priest of the early T'ang period named Tao-hsuan (Dōsen), whose disciples Ganjin studied under.

During the Kamakura period, the Ritsu sect was divided into schools at Tōshōdaiji, Kaidan'in, Saidaiji and Sen'yūji, each temple becoming an object of worship. However, as part of the Meiji government measures for dealing with Buddhism, the Ritsu sect was incorporated within the Shingon sect. Consequently, today only Tōshōdaiji, which resisted the measures, retains its identity as a Ritsu sect temple.

Q: What is the Shingon sect?

This is the sect which Kūkai (Kōbō Daishi) established upon returning from China with Buddhist images and scriptures. The main object of worship which Kūkai established was the Kongōbuji on Mt. Kōya, but subsequently the sect subdivided and now there are many sub-sects and objects of wor-

特に、12世紀に覚鑁(かくばん)(1095-1143)が出て、綱紀の緩んだ真言宗を立て直し、新義真言宗が成立したことは銘記すべきでしょう。この派から智積院(ちしゃくいん)を本山とする智山派(ちざんは)、長谷寺(ちょうこくじ)を本山とする豊山派(ぶざんは)ができて、今日に至るまで栄えています。

真言宗は、もともとインドに発生した密教といわれます。密教では従来の仏教を「顕教(けんぎょう)」と呼び、釈迦が衆生のためにやさしく説いた仮の教えだといいます。それに対して真実の仏は大日如来(にちにょらい)といい、森羅万象(しんらばんしょう)を通じて真理を説いているが、通常はそれが理解できないので「密教」というのです。

人はこの大日如来と特別なコミュニケーションをとることにより、この身このままで仏になることができるというのが密教の独特の教理です。これを「即身成仏(そくしんじょうぶつ)」といいます。

そのコミュニケーションの方法とは、手に印を結び、口に仏の言葉である真言を唱え、心に仏を念じることです。

真言宗がよりどころとしている経典は『大日経』と『金剛頂経』ですが、これを象徴的に図示したものが「曼荼羅(まんだら)」です。前者は「胎蔵曼荼羅(たいぞう)」、後者は「金剛界曼荼羅(こんごうかい)」と呼ばれ、両者を合わせて「両部曼荼羅(りょうぶ)」といいます。仏・菩薩たちの世界を描いたもので、信者たちの礼拝の対象となっています。

Q: 天台宗(てんだいしゅう)とはどんな宗派ですか?

平安時代、空海と同時期に、伝教大師最澄(でんぎょうだいしさいちょう)が中国からもたらし、日本に定着させた宗派で

ship.

It is especially worthy of note that in the 12th century Kakuban reestablished the Shingon sect, whose official discipline had grown rather lax. From this sect developed the Chizan branch which takes Chishakuin as its head temple and the Buzan branch which takes Chōkokuji as its main temple. Both are still prosperous today.

The Shingon sect is Esoteric Buddhism (Mikkyō) which is said to have arisen in India. In the Mikkyō sects, existing teachings are referred to as "exoteric Buddhism," which they say the Buddha preached as simplified, temporary Buddhism for the masses. In contrast, the true Buddha is *Dainichi Nyorai* (*Maha Vairocana*), who preaches the truth through all creation, but because it cannot ordinarily be understood, is referred to as "esoteric."

By means of establishing special communication with this *Dainichi Nyorai* (*Maha Vairocana*) one can become a buddha in one's very body. This is a distinctive doctrine of Esoteric Buddhism and is called *sokushin jōbutsu*.

Such communication is achieved by forming mudras with the hands, reciting mantras and keeping the Buddha in one's mind.

The Shingon sect takes as its central scriptures the *Mahavairocana Sutra* and *Vajrasekhara Sutra*, which are represented by mandalas. The former is the Womb Realm Mandala and the latter is the Diamond Realm Mandala, and together they are referred to as the Mandalas of the Two Realms. They portray the realm of the Buddhas and Bodhisattvas and are objects of veneration among believers.

Q: What is the Tendai sect?

This is the sect which was brought back from China and established in Japan by Saichō (Dengyō Daishi), who lived in

す。本山は比叡山延暦寺です。

　唐に渡った最澄は、天台山で天台宗の教義を
学びました。天台宗とは、6世紀、隋の天台大
師智顗（ちぎ）によって大成された宗派です。その思想
は『法華経』を最高の教えととらえ、あらゆる
人が仏になれると説いて、他者を仏の道に誘
い、自分も仏になる修行をしようというもので
す。だから最澄は、日本に帰ってから自分の宗
派を天台法華宗と名づけたのです。
　その修行法には、『梵網経（ぼんもうきょう）』という経典に載
っている戒律を受けることと、智顗の著した
『摩訶止観（まかしかん）』に説く精神を安定・集中させるこ
とがあります。いわば一種の禅ともいえると思
います。
　最澄はほかにも禅林寺（ぜんりんじ）で禅を学び、越州の竜
興寺（こうじ）で密教を学んで日本に伝えたため、比叡山
に、円（天台）・密（密教）・禅・戒という総
合仏教を樹立することになりました。
　その後、最澄の弟子の円仁（えんにん）が中国から浄土教
の念仏を伝え、その総合性はますます充実しま
す。鎌倉時代に至って、法然や親鸞などが新宗
派を作って比叡山から巣立っていく素地は、こ
こにあったのです。それから以後は多くの流派
を生み出し、歴史的な紆余曲折を経て今日に至
っています。

Q: 浄土宗（じょうどしゅう）とはどんな宗派ですか？

　　　鎌倉時代に法然（ほうねん）が開いた宗派です。総本山は
京都の知恩院、大本山は東京の増上寺（ぞうじょうじ）、京都の
金戒光明寺（こんかいこうみょうじ）、百万遍知恩寺、清浄華院（しょうじょうけいん）、久
留米（るめ）の善導寺（ぜんどうじ）、鎌倉の光明寺（こうみょうじ）、長野の善光寺（ぜんこうじ）

the Heian period with Kūkai. The main temple is Enryakuji on Mt. Hiei.

Saichō went to T'ang China and studied the doctrines of the T'ien-tai sect on Mt. T'ien-t'ai. It was a mature sect founded in the Sui period in the sixth century by Chih-i. It held the Lotus Sutra to be the ultimate teaching, and preaching that everyone can become a buddha, it promoted bringing others to the path of the Buddha and practicing together with them to become buddhas. Therefore, when Saichō returned from China, he called the sect that he founded the Tendai Lotus Sect.

As its methods of practice, it required obedience to the precepts and regulations in the *Brahmajala Sutra* (*Bommyō-kyō*) and the methods of meditation included in Chih-i's *Mohochihkuan* (*Makashikan*). It was in short a variety of Zen.

Because Saichō had also studied Zen at Zenrinji and Esoteric Buddhism at Ryūkōji and introduced these to Japan, he founded a comprehensive Buddhism at Mt. Hiei, composed of Tendai, Esoteric, Zen and rules of conduct.

Later, when Saichō's follower En'nin returned from China and introduced the *nembutsu* of Jōdo teachings, this comprehensiveness was further enriched. It is for this reason that through the Kamakura period Mt. Hiei provided the groundwork for such priests as Hōnen and Shinran to create new sects. From that time forth it has given birth to a large number of sects and continued through the vicissitudes of history to the present day.

Q: What is the Jōdo sect?

The Jōdo (Pure Land) sect was founded by Hōnen in the Kamakura period. The central temple is Chion'in in Kyōto and major temples include Zōjōji in Tōkyō; Konkaikōmyōji, Hyakumanben-Chionji and Shōjōkein in Kyōto; Zendōji in

知恩院
Chion'in

などです。

　法然は初め比叡山で勉学と修行の日々を送っていましたが、自分の力で修行し、悟りを開くことにどうしても限界と疑問を感じざるを得ませんでした。

　そんな時、法然は唐の善導が書いた『観無量寿経疏』というお経の注釈書を目にしました。そこには、阿弥陀仏がいっさいの衆生を救うという願いを立てて仏になったのだから、ほかの行は捨ててひたすら阿弥陀仏の名を称えて救ってもらいなさい、と書いてありました。

　法然はこの一文に感激し、自分の力で悟りを開く道を捨て、阿弥陀仏の力に頼り、「南無阿弥陀仏」と念仏を称えて仏の救済を信じる専修念仏の教えを開きました。これが浄土宗です。自力を捨て、仏の力を頼る他力を特徴としています。この教えは、自力では布施や修行などをすることができない庶民の圧倒的な支持を得て広まりました。

　浄土宗では、『無量寿経』『観無量寿経』『阿弥陀経』の３つを根本の聖典とし、「浄土三部経」と呼んで尊んでいます。

　法然の没後、弟子の信空や弁長、証空、親鸞などが教えを継承し、後にそれぞれ浄土宗、浄土宗西山派、浄土真宗として隆盛して現在に至っています。

Q: 浄土真宗とはどんな宗派ですか？

　法然の弟子である親鸞が開いた宗派です。現

Kurume; Kōmyōji in Kamakura; and Zenkōji in Nagano.

Hōnen in the beginning spent his days at Mt. Hiei studying and practicing, but he was unable to rid himself of doubts concerning his ability to practice and achieve enlightenment through his own powers.

It was at that time that he read an annotation of *The Meditation on the Buddha of Infinite Life Sutra* by Shan-tao. Since Amida Buddha had become a buddha pledging to save all sentient beings, it said, one should abandon all other practices and rely upon Amida for salvation by calling upon him.

Moved by this single verse, Hōnen propagated the teaching of exclusive reliance on the *nembutsu* meaning setting aside one's own powers in achieving enlightenment, depending upon the power of Amida Buddha, and believing in the attainment of salvation of the Buddha by intoning *"Namu Amida Butsu."* This is the Pure Land sect. It is characterized by casting aside one's own strength and depending on the strength of the other, that of the Buddha. This teaching obtained overwhelming, broad support from the common people who were unable with their own strength to make donations or practice austerities.

The Jōdo sect takes the *Buddha of Infinite Life Sutra*, the *Meditation on the Buddha of Infinite Life Sutra*, and the *Amida Sutra* as its fundamental scriptures and they are venerated as the "Triple Pure Land Sutras."

Following Hōnen's death, his disciples Shinkū, Benchō, Shokū and Shinran succeeded to his teachings, giving birth to the Jōdo sect, the Jōdo sect Seizan branch, and the Jōdo Shin sect which remain prominent today.

Q: What is the Jōdo Shin sect?

Hōnen's disciple Shinran founded the Jōdo Shin sect. In

在は、浄土真宗本願寺派と真宗大谷派に分か
れ、前者が西本願寺、後者が東本願寺を本山と
しています。

　法然が四国に流罪になった時、親鸞も今の新
潟に流されました。その後、赦免になり、越後
で結婚した恵信尼とともに関東の地に移り住ん
だころから、親鸞は独自の思想を形成していっ
たようです。
　『無量寿経』には、阿弥陀仏が仏となる前の、
まだ法蔵菩薩と名乗っていたころの物語がのっ
ています。そこには、法蔵菩薩は48の願を立
て、それが達成されないうちは仏にならないと
誓ったとあります。そしてそのうちの18願に、
あらゆる衆生が自分の浄土に生まれたいと欲
し、10回念じても生まれることができないなら
ば、自分は仏にならないとあります。

　親鸞はこの願に注目しました。阿弥陀仏はす
でに仏になっているのですから、この願は達成
されていることになります。つまり、阿弥陀仏
に対して信心さえ起こせば、私たちはもう救わ
れているのです。だから念仏は仏に対する報恩
感謝の念仏だとして、よけいな自力の行を徹底
して否定しました。ただ誠の信心を持った時に
救われるとして、絶対他力を説いたのです。

　親鸞の教えは、本願寺を通じて子孫が後世に
伝えていくことになりますが、8代の蓮如の
時、浄土真宗は爆発的に発展しました。その勢
力は権力者にも向けられて一向一揆を触発しま
すが、11代顕如の時、織田信長に弾圧されまし
た。その後、戦国時代の混乱の中で、浄土真宗
は東西の本願寺に分裂して今日に至るのです。

蓮如
Rennyo

the present day the sect is divided into the Jōdo Shinshū Hon-ganji branch, with Nishi Honganji as its main temple, and the Shinshō Ōtani branch, with Higashi Honganji as its main temple.

When Hōnen was banished to Shikoku, Shinran was sent to present-day Niigata. Afterwards when he was pardoned, Shinran moved with Eshin whom he had married in Echigo province to the Kantō area, and it seems that around this time he had formed his own way of thinking.

In the *Buddha of Infinite Life Sutra* is the story of Amida Buddha before he became a buddha and was still known as *Hōzō Bosatsu* (*Dharmakara*). It was while Amida was this bodhisattva that he made forty-eight vows and pledged not to become a buddha until he had fulfilled them. The eighteenth vow was to have all sentient beings born in his own Pure Land, and if he could not bring this about with ten prayers then he would not become a buddha.

Shinran focused on this vow. Amida had already become a buddha, which meant that the vow was already fulfilled. In other words, if we but have faith in Amida, we have already been saved. Taking the *nembutsu* as an invocation of gratitude to the Buddha, he categorically denied practices of "one's own power" as superfluous. He preached absolute reliance on "power of the other (=Amida)," such that one is saved when one achieves correct faith.

The teachings of Shinran were transmitted to posterity at Honganji, and with the appearance of Rennyo, the eighth head abbot, the Jōdo Shin sect witnessed dramatic growth. Its influence touched off uprisings of the common people against the authorities, but under the eleventh abbot Kennyo the sect was suppressed by Oda Nobunaga. During the subsequent period of warring states the Jōdo Shin sect split into the East and West Honganji factions which have remained to the present time.

Q: 日蓮宗とはどんな宗派ですか？

久遠寺
Kuonji

　　鎌倉時代に日蓮が開いた宗派です。総本山は身延山久遠寺（山梨県）です。

　　日蓮は比叡山で天台宗の教学を学びましたが、彼はその中から『法華経』という１つの経典のみを選び取りました。そしてこの経に帰依して「南無妙法蓮華経」と称えれば、すべての人が仏になることができると主張しました。それは、法然が「南無阿弥陀仏」と称えればだれでも救われると説いたのに似ています。たぶん影響があったのでしょう。

　　日蓮の主著に、『立正安国論』があります。彼はこの中で、天変地異や飢饉、疫病が蔓延し、死体が道に転がっている現状を悲しまないものはいない。これを打開するためには、国家をあげて『法華経』に帰依しなければならないと言っています。つまり、日蓮宗の教えは個人の救済もさることながら、さらに社会の救済に重きが置かれているところに特徴があるといえましょう。

　　日蓮の死後、六老僧といわれる高弟たちが仏法の伝統を継ぎますが、日蓮宗も時代とともに多くの流派に分かれ、それぞれの流派が興隆していくことになります。

　　戦後、日蓮宗の教えをベースにした新興宗教が次々とでき、エネルギーにあふれる活動を展開しましたが、その背景には、このような教義があったことを挙げることができるのではないでしょうか。

Q: What is the Nichiren sect?

This sect was founded by Nichiren during the Kamakura period. Its main temple is Minobusan Kuonji in Yamanashi prefecture.

Nichiren studied Tendai teachings at Mt. Hiei, and among them he selected the Lotus Sutra exclusively. He asserted that if anyone devoted himself to this sutra chanting *"Namu Myōhō Renge-kyō,"* he could become a buddha. This was similar to Hōnen's view that whoever intoned *"Namu Amida Butsu"* would be saved. Perhaps there was some influence.

Nichiren's main work was *Treatise on the Establishment of the True Dharma and the Peace of the Nation.* In it he wrote that there was no one who did not grieve over the current state in which natural calamities, famine and epidemics occurred in succession and corpses lay strewn on the streets. He claimed that the only way to resolve affairs was for the nation as a whole to pay homage to the *Lotus Sutra.* In sum, it can be said that while the teachings of the Nichiren sect are for the salvation of the individual, they also place weight on the salvation of society.

Following Nichiren's death, six senior priests were chosen to maintain his teachings, but as time passed the sect divided into many factions and these thrived.

Following the war, so-called "new religions" based on the teachings of Nichiren appeared in rapid succession and developed with vigorous activity. This is surely due to the nature of the teachings themselves.

Q: 時宗とはどんな宗派ですか?

一遍上人の開いた宗派。総本山は神奈川県藤沢市にある遊行寺こと、清浄光寺です。

一遍は法然の弟子筋にあたります。法然の直弟子であった親鸞が、阿弥陀仏への信心を強調したのに対し、一遍は、一度でも「南無阿弥陀仏」と念仏を唱えれば、信心があろうとなかろうと阿弥陀仏が救ってくれる、と考えました。

そこで人々を救済に導くため、全国を巡り歩いて「南無阿弥陀仏決定往生六十万人」と書いた札を配ったのです。この布教の方法は、一遍の宗派を受け継ぐ代々の上人に継承されています。

一遍は事物への執着を否定し、いっさいの財物を持たずに遊行を続けました。これを受け継ぐ弟子たちも、一遍の精神を受け継ぎ、皆、遊行上人と呼ばれています。

なお、時宗の特徴として「踊り念仏」を挙げておく必要があるでしょう。阿弥陀仏に救われる喜びを踊りで表現するもので、これが盆踊りのもとになったともいわれているのです。

一遍の死後は他阿真教が跡を継いで宗派の基礎を固め、以後、代々の宗主が他阿の名を継承して遊行を務めてきています。

Q: 臨済宗とはどんな宗派ですか?

栄西が中国から日本にもたらした禅の一宗です。流派は多くに分かれており、それぞれに本山があります。

栄西は、宋で虚庵懐敞に師事し、臨済禅を身

Q: What is the Ji sect?

This sect was founded by Ippen . Its main temple in Fuji-sawa, Kanagawa prefecture, is Yugyōji, also known as Shōjōkōji.

Ippen was a follower of Hōnen's disciples. Where Hōnen's direct disciple Shinran emphasized that one should have faith in Amida Buddha, Ippen felt that if one even once thought of the Buddha and chanted *"Namu Amida Butsu,"* whether one was sincere or not, Amida would offer salvation.

Then in order to bring people to salvation, he traveled throughout the land distributing talismans upon which were written, "Take refuge in Amida Buddha; definite rebirth; six hundred thousand believers." This method of propagation has been handed down through generations of eminent priests.

Ippen denied an attachment to material things and carrying absolutely no possessions he spent his life wandering. The disciples who accepted his teachings also accepted his spirit and all came to be mendicant priests.

A particular feature of the Ji sect is its *"nembutsu* dance," a dance which expresses the ecstasy of Amida's salvation. It is held by some to be the origin of the "Bon dances."

Following Ippen's death, Taashinkyō succeeded him and established the foundations of the sect. From that time forth the sect leader has taken the name Taa and followed the tradition of the mendicant wandering priesthood.

Q: What is the Rinzai sect?

Rinzai is a sect of Zen Buddhism which Eisai brought back from China. It is divided into many branches, each with its own main temple.

Eisai studied in China under Hsu-an Huai-ch'ang and mas-

建仁寺
Kenninji

につけました。帰国後は既成の教団の弾圧を受けますが、武士たちの帰依を受けて、鎌倉幕府に保護されました。そして、京都に建仁寺（けんにんじ）を開き、臨済宗を広めたのです。

　臨済宗は、もともと、中国の臨済義玄（りんざいぎげん）が起こしたものです。釈迦は菩提樹の下で坐禅を組んで悟りを開きましたが、禅宗の禅ではこれにならって坐禅を組み、煩悩（ぼんのう）を打ち払って、心を安定させるのです。

　臨済宗の特徴にはもう１つ、「公案」と言われることがあります。公案とはもともと、民の守るべき法案のことです。その意味が転じて人々のよるべき教理を指すようになり、また、高僧の言葉を言うようになったのです。この言葉を修行者に示し、真理を探究する手がかりとさせるのです。

　臨済宗は、鎌倉幕府の保護を受けておおいに栄えます。室町時代になるとその勢力はますます大きくなりました。そのためそれを秩序だて、統制する必要が生じ、主要な５つの寺、その下に10の寺、という形で、鎌倉や京都の寺に格付けをしました。これらの寺を中心に、禅僧たちによって漢文学が栄えました。

　以後、臨済宗は妙心寺派（みょうしんじ）を中心に受け継がれ、名僧・高僧が出て、そこからさらに多くの流派を形成していきました。

Q: 曹洞宗（そうとうしゅう）とはどんな宗派ですか？

　道元（どうげん）が中国から持ち来たった禅の宗派の１つです。大本山は福井県の永平寺（えいへいじ）と横浜市鶴見区の総持寺（そうじじ）です。

tered Lin-chi Ch'an (Rinzai Zen). When he returned to Japan, he suffered under pressure from existing religious orders, but he received followers from among the warrior class and gained the patronage of the Kamakura government. He constructed the Kenninji in Kyōto and expanded the Rinzai sect.

The Rinzai sect was originally founded by the Chinese master Lin-chi I-hsuan. The Buddha seated himself in meditation beneath a bodhi tree and achieved enlightenment, and the Zen sect followed this form by sitting in meditation, dispelling all illusions and achieving spiritual calm.

A further characteristic of the Rinzai sect is what is called the *koan*. A *koan* was originally a teaching that the people were to uphold. The meaning later changed so that it referred to doctrines that people could fall back on, and still later came to refer to sayings of eminent priests. This proposition is given to the practitioner for help in groping toward the truth.

Under the patronage of the Kamakura government the Rinzai sect flourished considerably. During the Muromachi period its influence grew even greater. It became necessary to establish some form of discipline and regulation, so the temples in Kamakura and Kyōto were arranged in a structure with five main temples with ten temples under each. With these temples as a focus, literature in the Chinese style flourished.

Thereafter, the Rinzai sect was handed down primarily through the Myōshinji faction, producing many eminent priests, from whom in turn developed a large number of branches.

Q: What is the Sōtō sect?

Sōtō Zen is the sect that Dōgen (1200-1253) brought back from China. Its main temples are Eiheiji in Fukui prefecture and Sōjiji in Tsurumi ward in Yokohama.

永平寺
Eiheiji

総持寺
Sōjiji

　道元は中国に渡り、如浄のもとで坐禅の極意を習得しました。この禅の本流は、洞山良价とその弟子の曹山本寂にまでさかのぼります。この2人の名前の1字ずつを取って、この禅は曹洞宗と呼ばれるようになったのです。

　曹洞宗には臨済宗のような公案はなく、ただひたすら坐禅することを教えます。坐禅は悟りを開くための修行ではなく、いっさいの考えを捨てて仏になりきることだというのです。この自分の姿が仏であると信じて、ひたすら座ること、道元はそのような坐禅を勧めています。

　道元は京都の宇治に興聖寺を開き、後に福井県の永平寺に居を移して、曹洞宗の考えを広めました。ところでその後、永平寺第4祖の瑩山禅師が能登（石川県）に総持寺を開き、さらに宗門の勢いを強めていったのです。そのため曹洞宗では道元を「高祖」、瑩山を「太祖」と仰ぎ、釈迦と併せて「一仏両祖」と呼んで尊びます。

　総持寺は明治31年に焼失し、現在の横浜の地に移されました。それで、曹洞宗には永平寺、総持寺という2つの本山があるのです。

Dōgen traveled to China, where he attained enlightenment through seated meditaion (*zazen*) under Ju-ching. The main tradition of this form of Zen goes back to Tung-shan Liang-chieh (Tōzan Ryōkai) and his disciple Ts'ao-shan Pen-chi (Sōzan Honjaku). The Japanese name of the sect was created by taking one character from each of their names.

Unlike the Rinzai sect, Sōtō has no *koan*s and teaches merely seated meditation. It holds that the purpose of seated meditation is not to achieve enlightenment, but rather to discard all thoughts and completely become a buddha. Dōgen promoted a seated meditation in which one simply sits and holds in mind the belief that one's own self is a buddha.

Dōgen founded Kōshōji in Uji near Kyōto, then later moved to Eiheiji in Fukui and disseminated the teachings of the Sōtō school. Eiheiji's fourth head abbot, Keizan, established a head temple in Noto, Ishikawa prefecture, strengthening the influence of the sect. Therefore, within the sect, Dōgen is venerated as the eminent founder (*kōso*), Keizan is honored as the founder (*taiso*), and together with the Buddha they are called "One Buddha and the Two Founders."

Sōjiji was destroyed by fire in 1898 and the head temple was moved to Yokohama where it remains now. That is why the Sōtō sect has two main temples, Eiheiji and Sōjiji.

6

寺と僧侶

Temples and Priests

Q: 寺はどのようにして発生してきたのですか？

　　釈迦は出家しました。「出家」とは文字通り
家を出ることですから、初めは釈迦もその弟子
たちも家を持たず、主に林や洞窟で修行してい
ました。

　　ところが、釈迦たちの指導を求める信者が、
修行道場を作って寄進するようになり、僧の定
住化が進むことになりました。この道場を「精
舎」といいました。これが寺の元祖と言うこと
ができるでしょう。

　　精舎は古代インドの言葉で「ヴィハーラ」ま
たは「サンガーラーマ」といい、このサンガー

Q: Where did temples come from?

The Buddha renounced the world. In Japanese, this is
expressed as "leaving one's home," and in the beginning the
Buddha and his disciples did not have homes, but mainly practiced exercises either in the forest or in caves.

However, the believers who came seeking their guidance
encouraged them to create a place for practice, and the priests
gradually began to take permanent residence. These places
were called *shōja*, and they are the ancestors of the temple.

The Indian word for these was *vihara* or *samgharama*.
The latter term was transliterated in Chinese as *sōgyaran*, and

ラーマを中国で「僧伽藍」と音写したところか
ら、僧院を伽藍と呼ぶようになったのです。

「寺」とはもともと、中国で外国の使者を泊め
る役所のことでした。インドの僧が初めて中国
に仏教を伝えた時、鴻臚寺という役所に泊まっ
たところから、後に僧侶の住居を寺というよう
になったと伝えられています。

538 年、仏教は朝鮮の百済から初めて日本に
もたらされましたが、その時に献上された仏像
を、蘇我稲目が大和向原の家に祀りました。わ
が国ではこれが最初の寺とされています。

なお、日本語の「寺」という言葉は、長老を
表す古代インドの「テーラ」、または礼拝所を
意味する朝鮮の「チョル」という言葉の転化だ
といわれています。

Q: 寺にはよく五重の塔がありますが、なんのためにある のですか?

五重の塔
Five-storied
pagoda

一言でいえば、仏を祀るためです。インドに
はもともと輪廻転生の思想があって、生き物は
すべて、死んではまた生まれ変わる、と考えら
れています。ですから、通常、死者を弔う墓や
塔は作られません。作っても、死者はすでに別
の生き物に生まれ変わっているからです。

ところが、解脱を果たした聖者に関しては別
です。釈迦が入滅した時、その遺骨は8つに分
けられ、遺体を焼いた灰とかめと合わせて10ヵ
国に分配されたといいます。そしてそれぞれの
国は塔を建て、それらを祀りました。これが仏
塔の初めといっていいでしょう。この塔はイン
ドでは「ストゥーパ」と呼ばれ、日本語の「卒
塔婆」の語源となっています。

monasteries came to be called *gyaran.*

The character for "temple" in China originally meant an administration building where foreign envoys stayed. When Indian priests for the first time introduced Buddhism to China, they stayed in a government building called Kōroji, and tradition says that thereafter the residences of monks and priests became known as "*ji,*" or temple.

Buddhism first came to Japan in 538 via Paekche on the Korean Peninsula, and the Buddhist images presented at that time were enshrined by Sogano Iname in the residence in Yamato Mukuhara. This is held to be the first temple in Japan.

The Japanese word "*tera*" is said to come from an Indian word "*thera*" meaning "elder" or from a Korean word "*chyol*" meaning "place of worship."

Q: Temples often have pagodas, but what are they for?

In short, they venerate the Buddha. In India people believed in reincarnation, which is the belief that all living things die and are then reborn. So normally no grave or monument was erected to mourn the dead. Even if one built a memorial, the dead person would already be reincarnated in another living being.

However, it was a different case with a holy man who had achieved emancipation. When the Buddha entered nirvana, it is said that his remains were divided into eight parts and that his ashes were placed in urns and distributed to ten countries. In these countries monuments were built and worshipped. These are the first Buddhist monuments. In India they were called *stupa,* which is the origin of the Japanese term *sotoba.*

　　形は最初は鉢を伏せたようなものだったので
すが、時代とともに変化し、だんだん筒状にな
っていきました。これが中国に入ると、鉢の上
方が縮小され、次第に四角や八角になっていき
ます。中国でもっとも古い仏塔は河南省にある
嵩山寺で、十二角十五重の塔だといいます。

　　日本では、蘇我馬子が大野丘に建てたものが
最初とされ、法隆寺の五重の塔は世界最古の木
造塔として有名です。

　　仏教では、あらゆる物質は地・水・火・風・
空という五大元素からできていると考えまし
た。これを「五大」といいます。塔を五重にす
るのは、人が死ねばこの元素に還元されるとい
うことで、五大を象徴しているのです。

Q: 寺はどうやって収入を得ているのですか？

　　基本的には、「布施」によっています。

　　出家するということは、俗の生活を捨てて聖
の生活に入ることです。具体的にいえば、利益
を求める生産活動を離れて、真理を追究する修
行に励むということです。

　　とはいえ、修行者といえども食べなければ死
んでしまいます。そこで釈迦とその弟子たち
は、托鉢によって命をつなぐ食を得ていまし
た。托鉢とは、僧が在家の信者の家々を回り、
食べ物などの施しを受けることです。

　　しかし、これには一定の作法が厳しく決めら
れていて、布施は一種の修行ということができ
ます。持って回る鉢は、その材料や色、大きさ
などが決められており、午前中1回だけに限ら
れましたし、また、必要以上のものを受けても
いけません。この伝統は、今でも禅の教団など

In the beginning they were shaped like a bowl turned upside down, but they changed through the ages, gradually turning cylindrical. When they reached China, the upper portion of the cylinder was shrunk, and they gradually assumed a quadragonal or hectagonal shape. In China the oldest extant tower is the twelve-sided, fifteen-story pagoda at Kōzanji in Henan.

The oldest in Japan is held to be the one built by Soga no Umako on Ōnogaoka, and the five-story pagoda at Hōryūji is famous as the world's oldest wooden tower.

In Buddhism all matter is believed to be composed of the five elements: earth, water, fire, wind, air. They are called "the five great (elements)." The five stories of the pagoda are symbolic of these five elements to which a person is restored after death.

Q: How do temples obtain income?

Fundamentally they depend on "donations."

By renouncing the world, priests cast aside the secular life and enter the religious life. In concrete terms, this means separating oneself from productive activity in pursuit of profit and devotion to practices in pursuit of truth.

Nonetheless, even a practitioner will die unless he or she eats. The Buddha and his disciples, therefore, obtained food for subsistence by begging for alms. To receive "alms" a priest goes from house to house of lay believers accepting donations of food and other things.

This receiving of alms has a formal etiquette which is firmly established, and donations can be said to be a variety of practice. The bowl that a priest carries has to be a certain size and of a certain material and color. Begging is limited to one time a day, in the morning, and one must not accept more than is necessary. Zen orders and others still follow this tradition.

に受け継がれています。

　時代は変わって、いやおうなく、寺も現代の社会機構の中に組み込まれざるを得ませんが、僧が信者に法を説き、信者の布施によって、寺が成り立っていることに変わりはありません。しかし、今は主に法事を通じて布施が行われ、寺が維持されていることが多いようです。

　とはいえ、これは檀家がいる菩提寺と呼ばれる寺の場合で、寺にはほかに、祈祷を専門にして、祈祷料で維持している寺、坐禅など修行の場を提供して布施を受ける寺、また観光の拝観料で維持する寺などがあります。

Q: 僧とはいったいどんな存在ですか？

　出家し、仏の教えを悟り、仏の教えを人々に伝える者のことです。

　釈迦の教団は、古代インドの言葉で「サンガ」と呼ばれていました。これは「共和国」や「組合のギルド」を意味します。釈迦はそれらの組織に、人々の和の姿を見出し、それを理想として自分の教団にその名を取り入れたのです。だから、サンガは「衆」とか「和合衆」と漢語で訳されます。修行僧たちの団体を指すわけです。

　ところで中国では、このサンガを「僧伽」と音写しました。そして、これが省略されて「僧」といわれるようになったのです。

　後世、中国や日本では、もともと団体を表したこの僧という言葉を、その団体を構成する個々人を指して言うようになりました。すなわ

Times have changed, and whatever reluctance one may have, the temple has had to become a part of the framework of society, but the fact that priests still preach the law to believers and the temple exists on the donations of those adherents has not changed. However, it does appear that many temples are now maintained primarily by donations for religious ceremonies.

Still, this is mostly the case of the so-called *bodaiji* temples which are "family temples." There are other temples which are supported by fees for offering prayers, temples which receive donations for providing a place to practice *zazen*, and some which accept admission fees for sightseeing purposes.

Q: What exactly is a priest?

A priest is one who leaves the secular world, *awakens* to the teachings of the Buddha and preaches the teachings to others.

The Buddha's group of followers were called *samgha* in India. It meant "republic" or "guild." The Buddha detected within these organizations the harmonious nature of the people involved, and taking that as an ideal, he adopted it as the name of his own order. Therefore, *samgha* is translated in Chinese style as "host" or "harmonious populace." It indicates the religious order comprised of practitioner priests.

In China *samgha* was transliterated as *sōgya*, and it was eventually abbreviated to simply "*sō*."

Later on in both China and Japan, this word "*sō*" which originally specified the group gradually came to be used in referring to the individuals who make up that group. In other

ち、出家した男性のことです。出家した女性は
「尼」とか「尼僧」と呼ばれます。

仏教では、仏と、その教えである法と、法を
実践し人々に伝える僧とを、3つの宝、すなわ
ち「三宝」といって尊んでいます。その三宝の
1つが僧なのです。

Q: 僧になる（出家する）ことに、どういう意味があるのですか？

釈迦は、欲望や執着を断ち切るために出家し
ました。
在家にとどまるということは、生産活動に従
事することです。それは、生産性を向上させな
ければならないことを意味します。そこには損
得といった世間的な価値観が生じます。在家で
いるということは、得、つまり欲を追求しなけ
ればならないのです。
また、家や職場では人間関係のしがらみに縛
られ、世間レベルのものの見方が要求されま
す。それに、家族や友人には愛情がわきますか
ら、どうしても彼らに執着してしまいます。

釈迦はそれらの欲や執着が苦を生み、真理を
見る目を覆い隠すと考えて出家したのです。で
すから、釈迦はほかの人にも出家を勧め、悟り
に導こうとしました。ですから出家には、欲望
や執着を断ち切って悟りを目指す、という意味
があるのです。
しかし釈迦は、在家の生活をすべて否定した
わけではありません。在家の信者も、戒を守っ
て善行を積めば、天界に生まれると教えたので
す。だが、悟りを開いて解脱を果たすためには

words, it refers to men who have renounced the world. Women who have left the secular world are called *ama* or *nisō*.

In Buddhism, the Buddha, the Law which is his teachings and the priests who practice the Law and transmit it to the people are together called and revered as *sambō* (three treasures or three jewels).

Q: What does it mean to become a priest (renounce the world)?

The Buddha renounced the world in order to sever the bonds of desire and attachment.

To remain in the lay (secular) world means to engage in productive activity. That means one has to improve productivity, and from this arises the secular value of profit and loss. Being in the secular world means that one has to pursue profit, in other words, one has desire.

Furthermore, in the family and the workplace one is bound by the ties of human relations and one needs to see things at the level of the society. Within the fabric of society there arises affection for family and friends, and attachment to them naturally arises.

The Buddha, thinking that such desire and attachment gave rise to suffering and obstructed vision of the truth, left the secular world. Therefore he encouraged others to forsake the world and led them toward enlightenment. That is why taking orders aims at enlightenment and the severing of the bonds of desire and attachment.

However, the Buddha did not deny all of the life of the laity. He taught that if lay believers obeyed the precepts and accumulated good works they too would be reborn in heaven. However, in order to achieve enlightenment and salvation, it

やはり出家することが必要だとされました。

　しかし、大乗仏教の時代になると様子は変わってきます。大乗仏教では、仏道を志すものは、出家であろうと在家であろうと同じ菩薩である、と考えられたからです。だれでも仏になることができるのですから、出家者は自分の悟りを追究し、同時に在家の人をも仏道に誘う指導者の役割に変わったといえるでしょう。

Q: 戒律とはなんですか？

　　仏教徒の守るべき規範です。

　正確にいえば、戒と律とは別の概念です。「戒」とは仏教に帰依した者が守るべきモラルで、罰則などはありません。インドの原語で「シーラ」といい、反復して身につける習慣をいいます。仏教徒としての善行を生活の中で繰り返し行い、身につけるべきことをいうのでしょう。

　仏教では、在家信者が守るべき「五戒」が示されています。それは次の５つです。

（１）不殺生……殺すなかれ。

（２）不偸盗……盗むなかれ。

（３）不邪淫……妻以外の女性とみだらなセックスをするなかれ。

（４）不妄語……うそをつくなかれ。

（５）不飲酒……酒を飲むなかれ。

　ユダヤ教・キリスト教には「十戒」がありますが、５番目の「酒を飲むなかれ」という戒めを除いて、あとの４つが共通しているのは興味深い事実です。

　一方、「律」とは、僧が守るべき規則で、こ

was deemed necessary to renounce the world.

During the period of Mahayana Buddhism, however, the situation changed. Within Mahayana, anyone who became a priest or remained a layperson was equally considered a bodhisattva because the person had set out upon the Buddha's path. Anyone was capable of becoming a buddha, so those who had taken orders were seen to seek their own enlightenment and at the same time they came to be seen as guides leading the laity to the Buddhist path.

Q: What are "precepts" (*kairitsu*)?

Precepts are standards that Buddhist followers must maintain.

More accurately there are two separate elements. "*Kai*" refers to the moral standards that those who are devoted to the Buddha ought to obey and it includes no rules for punishment. The original Indian word is *sila*, meaning a habit one attains via reiteration. So it may be seen as good acts which a Buddhist follower ought to carry out in his daily life making them part of himself.

In Buddhism there are "five precepts" which lay believers ought to abide by.
(1) Abstain from destruction of life
(2) Abstain from stealing
(3) Abstain from having sex with a woman other than one's wife
(4) Abstain from lying
(5) Abstain from intoxicants

The fact that with the exception of the fifth precept, concerning abstinence, these precepts are common to the Ten Commandments of Judaism and Christianity is of profound interest.

The element "*ritsu*" refers to the regulations that the

ちらには罰則規定があります。僧たちが悪い行いをするたびに釈迦がそれを禁じる規則を決めていったものです。経蔵、論蔵と並んで、仏教の聖典を構成する三蔵の1つになっています。

仏教が中国に移入されると、この戒と律が混同されてしまいます。「戒律」という言葉で一くくりにされてしまったのです。それを中国で初めて整理・体系化したのが、初唐の高僧・南山律師道宣です。日本に律を伝えた鑑真は、この道宣の孫弟子にあたります。

Q: 僧が髪を剃るのはなぜですか？

いっさいの世間的な虚飾を捨てるためです。経典には、釈迦が家族を捨て、カピラ城を脱出して出家を果たした時、自分で髪を切って、道を求めることを誓ったと書いてあります。このへんが由来なのでしょうか。

また、次のような説もあります。釈迦は悟りを開いたあと、最初に、以前いっしょに修行をしていた5人の仲間を訪ねたといいます。5人は初め、苦行を捨てた釈迦を堕落者と決めつけ、無視しようと思っていました。

ところが、一目、釈迦の姿を見た時、5人はその神々しさに打たれ、釈迦の説法に耳を傾けました。そして一言教えを聞いた瞬間、尊い言葉に感激して、その場にひれ伏しました。その時、衝撃で彼らの髪のもとどりが解けたというのです。そして、これが剃髪のもとになったというのですが、おそらく伝説でしょう。

いずれにしても、飾りを捨て、また、ほかの

priests are required to obey, and here there are provisions for punishment. Each time the priests performed some wrong deed, the Buddha established a rule that prohibited it. This group of regulations called *ritsuzō* (*vinaya*) together with the Buddha's teachings, called *kyōzō* (*sutra*) and *ronzō* (*abhidharma*) compose the three branches of Buddhist scriptures called *Sanzō* (*tripitaka*).

When Buddhism was introduced to China, these "precepts" and "regulations" had become merged and ended up lumped together. In China for the first time they were organized and systematized by the early T'ang priest Tao-hsuan (Dōsen). Ganjin, who transmitted the regulations to Japan was a follower of Tao-hsuan's disciples.

Q: Why do priests shave their heads?

This is done to cast aside all secular ostentations. In the scriptures it is written that when the Buddha actually renounced the world by casting aside his family and extricating himself from Kapila Palace, he cut his own hair and vowed to seek the path. This is the likely source of the custom.

Another theory says that when the Buddha attained awakening, the first thing he did was to visit the five companions he had previously practiced with. In the beginning the five had called him to task for having cast aside austerities and they ignored him.

However, when the five saw the Buddha's awe-inspiring appearance, they gave careful attention to what he preached. And when they heard one word of what he said, they were moved by his marvelous teachings and immediately prostrated themselves. It is said that at that moment their topknots came undone. This is the legend behind the shaving of the head.

At any rate, it is said that the head is shaved to cast aside

宗教の行者と区別をするために、剃髪が行われるといわれています。

Q: 袈裟にはどういう意味があるのですか？

僧は、欲望や執着を捨てるために出家します。だから、釈迦の弟子たちは三衣一鉢といって、ごく限られたものしか所有することができませんでした。

彼らの着るものは「糞掃衣」といい、道や墓場などに捨てられたものや人からもらったものでした。そういうものしか身につけることを許されなかったのです。

彼らは、道や墓場で拾ってきた布を縫い合わせて身にまといました。それを古代インドの言葉で「カーシャーヤ」といいます。「色の混じった」という意味です。このカーシャーヤが「袈裟」と音写され、今日に伝わっているわけです。

後に仏教教団が分裂すると、部派によって色や形に変化が生じました。そのため、部派仏教が伝わった東南アジアの諸国では、現在も国によってある程度、色や形が違うのです。

中国や日本では、時代が経つにしたがって、袈裟は儀式用として作られるようになっていきました。そのためだんだんと華美になり、用途や宗派によっては、複雑で豪華なものになってきたのです。

現在の日本では、僧の位によって色や形が違いますし、また儀式によって着る袈裟の種類を替えます。時代とともに、本来の袈裟の意味とはだいぶ変質してしまったといえるでしょう。

正装した僧
Dressed-up
Buddhist priest

any adornment and also to distinguish practitioners from those of other religions.

Q: What is the symbolism of the Buddhist surplice (*kesa*)?

A priest takes orders in order to cast aside desire and attachment. Therefore, the followers of the Buddha were only allowed to have limited possessions referred to as "three robes and one bowl."

This clothing, called *funzōe* (*pamsu-kula*), were items cast aside at the roadside or the graveyard or things which they received from others. That was all they were allowed to wear.

They covered themselves in clothing made from scraps they picked up on the streets or in cemeteries. The Indian word for this was *kasaya*, meaning "of mixed colors." The word comes down to us today as the transliteration *kesa*.

Later, when the Buddhist order fragmented, the various groups took on their own colorings and froms. As a result, in each of the countries of Southeast Asia to which sectarian Buddhism was transmitted, it has a different coloration and design.

In China and Japan, with the passage of time the surplice came to be made for ceremonial purposes. For that reason, the surplice gradually became more colorful, and depending on the use and the sect, they have become more complex and gorgeous.

In present-day Japan, the color and the shape differ with the position of the priest who wears it, and there are different surplices for each ceremony. It can surely be said that a transformation occurred over time from the original meaning of the *kesa*.

Q: 数珠はなんのために持つのですか?

　仏や菩薩を礼拝するために、手にかけて用います。珠の数を利用して念仏の回数を数えるためにも用います。

　起源はよくわかりませんが、かなり古いらしく、インド古代のバラモンが使っていたようです。したがってヒンドゥー教でも用いられています。これが西洋に伝わり、ローマ教会の数珠であるロザリオになったといいますし、またイスラム教でもインド風の数珠が用いられています。

　仏教の場合、通常は108の珠が輪状につないでありますが、これは煩悩の数が108あることにちなんでいると言われています。ただし宗派やものによっては、その半分の54、さらにその半分の27のもの、また36や18の珠のものもあります。

　「じゅじゅ」や「ずず」などとも読まれ、また、珠を1つまさぐるごとに、仏を念ずるところから、念珠とも呼ばれます。珠は菩提樹の実、水晶などで作られます。仏教徒にとってはもっとも身近な仏具といえるでしょう。

Q: Why do they carry a string of beads?

The string of beads is placed over the hands when worshipping the Buddha or bodhisattva. The beads are also used for counting the *nembutsu*.

It is not exactly clear what the origin of the beads is, but it appears they were used quite early in the Brahman religion of ancient India. Consequently, they are also used in the Hindu religion. It is thought that they were introduced to the West, eventually becoming the "rosary" of the Roman Catholic Church. Moreover, an Indian-style string of beads is also used in Islam.

In Buddhism, there are usually 108 beads strung together, and this is held to come from the 108 illusions. However depending on the sect, the number may be half of this number (54), a quarter (27), a third (36) or a sixth (18).

The character for this string of beads can also be read *juju* or *zuzu* and may also be called *nenju*. The "*ju*" portion is the seed of the bodhi tree, and is made of such things as crystal. It is probably the most familiar Buddhist accessory from the point of view of Buddhists.

仏教と庶民の生活・行事

Buddhism and the Life and Ceremonies of the People

Q: 仏教では、人が死んだあとのことをどう考えていますか？

　　　仏教の発祥の地インドでは、今でも、あらゆる生き物は死んでもまた生まれ変わり、何度も生死を繰り返すと信じられています。仏教もこの考え方を取り入れ、私たちは次の6つの世界に生まれ変わるとしました。

　　　すなわち、地獄界（道）・餓鬼界（道）・阿修羅界（道）・畜生界（道）・人界（道）・天界（道）の6つです。この6つの世界を「六道」と呼んでいます。

　　　すべての生あるものは、生前の行いによっ

Q: In Buddhism, what happens after a person dies?

In India where Buddhism arose, even now the people believe that when every living thing dies it is reborn and that life and death are repeated time and again. Buddhism accepted this way of thinking and held that we are reborn in the following six worlds.

These "six paths," as they are called, include the realms of hell, hungry spirits, asuras, animals, humans and heavenly beings.

All living beings upon death are reborn in one of these

て、死ぬと、この6つの世界のいずれかに生まれ変わります。これを「輪廻転生」とか「六道輪廻」と呼びます。 しかし、これらの世界はいずれも苦しみの世界だといわれています。喜びと快楽に満ちた天人の世界でさえ、老死を免れ得ない苦の世界なのです。

　ただし2つだけ、これら苦の世界を脱出する方法があります。1つは煩悩を滅して涅槃に入ることであり、もう1つは、仏の力を頼み、浄土に往生することです。そして、浄土で仏道の修行をして悟りを開き、仏となるのです。

　私たちは、死後これらのいずれかの道を歩むことになるわけです。

Q: 地獄とはどんなところですか？

　悪事を犯した人が死んでから生まれ変わる、最悪の苦しみの世界です。地獄には、大きく分けて2つあります。
（1）八大熱地獄
（2）八大寒地獄
　このうち、なんといっても有名なのは八大熱地獄のほうでしょう。熱地獄に落ちた人は、熱風の中、牛頭、馬頭と呼ばれる鬼たちに刑罰を受けることになります。次の8つの刑罰です。

地獄図
Picture of hell

（1）等活地獄……鬼に鉄棒でたたきつぶされます。
（2）黒縄地獄……体に墨縄で線を引かれ、線に沿って切られます。
（3）衆合地獄……かみそりのような葉のある木に、何度も上り下りさせられます。
（4）叫喚地獄……口から溶けた銅を流し込まれます。
（5）大叫喚地獄……上の10倍の苦しみを受

realms depending on their acts while they were alive. This is called "transmigration of the soul" or "transmigration within the six realms." However, each of these six worlds is held to be a world of suffering. Even the realm of heavenly beings, which is filled with joy and pleasure, is a realm of suffering in that it is not exempt from old age and death.

There are two ways to escape from this world of suffering. One is to extinguish all illusions and enter nirvana. The other is to depend upon the power of the Buddha and be reborn in the Pure Land, where one practices the way of the Buddha, achieves enlightenment, and becomes a buddha.

Therefore, when we die, we take one of these two paths.

Q: What kind of place is hell?

Hell is a world of the worst suffering to which people who committed evil acts while alive are reborn. Hell is roughly divided into two parts.

(1) Eight hot hells
(2) Eight cold hells

Of these, the eight hot hells are the more widely known. Those who fall into these hells are tortured in the midst of intense heat by demons with non-human heads. The eight punishments are as follows

(1) *Tōkatsu-jigoku*, where one is beaten and smashed by demons with iron clubs
(2) *Kokujō-jigoku*, where one's body is marked with a carpenter's line and then sliced along those lines
(3) *Shugō-jigoku*, where one is made to repeatedly go up and down a tree with leaves like razors
(4) *Kyōkan-jigoku*, where molten metal is poured down one's throat
(5) *Daikyōkan-jigoku*, where one receives ten times the pain as

けます。
（6）焦熱地獄……かまやなべで煮られ、肛
　　門から頭へ鉄串を刺されて焼かれます。

（7）大焦熱地獄……焦熱地獄の10倍の苦し
　　みを受けます。
（8）阿鼻地獄……間断なく責め苦を受ける
　　ので、無間地獄ともいわれます。

　八大寒地獄のほうは、うってかわって極寒の
世界です。寒さのために歯の根も合わず、さま
ざまな凍傷にかかって体が崩れるのです。
　いずれの地獄にしても、さらに恐ろしいのは
気の遠くなるような長い刑期です。

Q: 極楽浄土とはどんなところですか？

　まず「浄土」について説明しましょう。仏に
なる前の菩薩は、自分が仏になったら、こんな
世界を作って人々を救い取りたい、と願をかけ
ます。その菩薩が仏になり、誓願が達成されて
できあがった国が「浄土」なのです。だから、
浄土とは仏たちのそれぞれの国のことです。

　極楽浄土は、阿弥陀仏という仏の国です。阿
弥陀仏がまだ法蔵という名の菩薩だった時、48
の願を立てて作った浄土です。
　極楽浄土は、西方十万億の仏土を過ぎたとこ
ろにあるといわれています。一仏土は、この太
陽系くらいの世界だと思ってください。それの
十万億倍も西のほうへ行ったところにあるので
す。
　この世界に生まれた人は、計り知れない光と
寿命を身に備えるといいます。衣食住の心配は
まったくありません。

above

(6) *Shōnetsu-jigoku*, where one is boiled in a pot or caldron and fried with an iron skewer sticking from the anus through the head

(7) *Daishōnetsu-jigoku*, where one receives ten times the pain as above.

(8) *Abi-jigoku*, also called *Muken-jigoku*, where one receives anguish without interruption

The eight cold hells are just the opposite, a world of extreme cold. Due to the cold, the teeth chatter, and the body suffers various kinds of frostbite and crumbles.

Whichever the hell, what is more frightening is the unfathomably long term of the sentence one serves there.

Q: What kind of place is the Pure Land?

First of all, let's look at the word "Jōdo" (Pure Land). The bodhisattva Amida, before he became a buddha, pledged that when he became a buddha, he would create such a world to save and receive people into. The world which this bodhisattva had vowed to create became the "Pure Land" when he attained buddhahood. Therefore the Pure Land is the various worlds of the buddhas.

The Pure Land is Amida Buddha's world. When Amida was still a bodhisattva named Hōzō, he made forty-eight vows and built the Pure Land.

The Paradise of the Pure Land is said to be 10,000,000,000,000 buddha-worlds to the west. If one buddha-world can be considered to be the size of our solar system, then it would be ten trillion times that distance to the west.

Those who are born into this world are said to be possessed of immeasurable light and lifetimes. They have absolutely no need to be concerned about clothing, food or

美しい七宝の池があって、池にはさまざまな
蓮華が咲き乱れ、いい香りが漂っています。す
ばらしい音楽が聞こえてきて、天からは美しい
花が降ってきます。

このような環境の中で、人々は阿弥陀仏の説
法を聴き、自分も仏となるべく修行に励んでい
るのです。いわば、仏教の理想の修行道場とい
えるでしょう。

Q: 仏教ではどうしてお墓を作るのですか？

仏教が入ってくる以前、古代の日本人は、死
者はやがてよみがえって生者に災いをもたらす
もの、と考えていました。そこで、人が死ぬと
穴を掘って埋め、その上に大きな石を乗せた
り、死者に石を抱かせたかっこうで埋葬したり
していました。よみがえらないように、遺体を
閉じ込めようとしたわけです。

ところが、やがて仏教が伝わってくると、火
葬が行われるようになりました。法相宗の開祖
道昭を遺言によって荼毘に付したのが、我が国
の火葬の始まりといわれています。

インドでは一般に遺体を火葬にしますが、墓
は作りません。そのようなインドの風習と日本
古来の葬送法が結びつき、火葬にした遺骨を土
中に埋め、お墓を造るようになったようです。

ただし、火葬にされるのはごく一部の人だけ
で、普通は土葬が中心でした。葬法には儒教の
影響なども加わり、また地域や身分などによっ
て複雑に混じり合った慣習ができてきました。

石塔が建てられるようになったのは平安時代
以降で、形もいろいろな過程を経て、現在見ら

shelter.

There is said to be a seven-jeweled lake filled with various kinds of blooming lotuses and a wonderful fragrance drifting everywhere. One can hear exquisite music and beautiful flowers come down from heaven.

In such surroundings, the people listen to the preachings of Amida Buddha and devote themselves to practice in order to become a buddha themselves. In sum, it is the ideal place to practice the teachings of Buddhism.

Q: In Buddhism, why does one make a grave?

Before the introduction of Buddhism, ancient Japanese thought that the dead returned to life and visited curses upon the living. Therefore, when someone died, people dug a hole, buried the body, and either put a large stone on top of it or buried the person embracing a large stone. They wanted to confine the body to ensure the body would not rise up again.

When Buddhism was introduced, cremation came to be practiced. Dōshō, founder of the Hosso sect who requested that his body be burned, is thought to be the first person cremated in Japan.

In India bodies are usually cremated and there are no graves. The Indian custom became tied with the ancient Japanese custom such that the cremated remains were buried in the earth and a monument was put up.

However, only certain groups of the people were cremated, and ordinarily interment was the rule. As to the ceremonies involved, there was influence from Confucianism and with differences according to region and social status, a complex mixture of customs evolved.

It was following the Heian period that stone monuments came to be erected, and there were various shapes over time,

れるようなものになっています。ただ、かつて
は石塔を建てたのは貴族や武士、僧などの墓で
あって、一般庶民にも広まってきたのは、江戸
時代になってからのことといわれています。

Q: 葬式後、四十九日とか三回忌とか、何度も法事をするのはなぜですか？

仏教では、人は死ぬとまた六道世界に生まれ
変わるといいますが、死んだ瞬間に生まれ変わ
るわけではありません。それなりの時間と手続
きが必要です。その手続きには四十九日という
日にちを要します。

この現世とも来世ともいえない中途半端な四
十九日の期間を、「中陰（ちゅういん）」または「中有（ちゅうう）」とい
います。人は死ぬとまず中陰の世界に入り、そ
の薄暗い世界を旅します。これを「冥土（めいど）の旅」
といいます。そして、7日ごとに7人の裁判官
のところに着き、7回の裁判を受けます。生前
の罪が審査され、その人が次に生まれ変わると
ころが検討されるのです。

だから遺族は、裁判の日ごとに法事をし、裁
判で死者が有利になるようにこの世から応援す
るのです。これを「回向（えこう）」といいます。

閻魔大王
The Great
King Emma

最初の裁判の日が初七日であり、以後7日ご
とに四十九日まで続きます。そして四十九日目
が最終判決の日となり、次に生まれるところが
決定されます。それで四十九日目を「満中陰（まんちゅういん）」
といい、特別な法事を行うのです。

かの有名な閻魔（えんま）大王も、この7人の裁判官の
中のひとりです。閻魔さまといえば、冥土の王
のようなイメージがありますが、実は7人の裁
判官の中の5番目の裁判官にすぎないのです。

until the present form evolved. Earlier it was only the nobility, the warrior class and the priesthood which put up monuments and had graves, and it was only in the Edo period that the custom spread to the general populace.

Q: Why are Buddhist services held so often, for example on the 49th day and the third anniversary after death?

Buddhism holds that after a person dies he or she is reborn in the "six realms," but not reborn at the exact moment of death. There is a certain process which requires forty-nine days.

The period of forty-nine days which is passed in a netherworld, neither the present world nor the next, is called "*chūin*" or "*chūu*." When one dies, one enters this intermediate state and travels through this shadowy realm. This is called "traveling to the world of the dead." Every seven days one comes before one of seven judges and receives a judgment. One's acts while alive are investigated, and where one will next be reborn is considered.

Therefore the bereaved hold a ceremony on each of the judgment days, lending support in this world so that the dead person might receive favor in the judgments. This is called "ekō," the transfer of merit.

The first judgment is on the seventh day, and this continues every seven days until the forty-ninth. The forty-ninth day is the day of the final verdict, when the world one will be reborn into is decided. The forty-ninth day is called "*manchūin*" and a special ceremony is held on this day.

The familiar *Enmadaiō*, *Yama* in Sanskrit, is one of these seven judges. *Enmadaiō* is usually recognized as being lord of the realm of the dead, but actually he is merely the fifth of these seven judges. There may even be judges more severe

閻魔大王より厳しい裁判官がまだまだいるということでしょうか。冥土の旅も楽ではありません。

この風習がインドから中国に伝わると、百ヵ日、一周忌、三回忌がつけ加えられます。さしずめ再審のチャンスとでもいえるでしょう。

こうして中国で十仏事といわれる法事が成立したのですが、これが日本に来るとさらに七回忌、十三回忌、三十三回忌が加えられて、十三回の仏事となり、それが普及して今日に至るのです。

Q: 仏壇はいつごろから家に置かれるようになったのですか?

現在、仏具屋さんでは、3月27日を「仏壇の日」としているそうです。それにはわけがあります。

我が国最古の公式な歴史書である『日本書紀』には、天武天皇が詔勅を下し、全国の公家の家に仏殿を作り、仏像や経典を安置せよと命じたと書いてあります。その詔勅の日が685年3月27日であり、この日が仏壇の発祥の日とされたのです。

仏壇
Family Buddhist
altar

ですから、最初はお寺や貴族の家に仏壇があっただけで、庶民レベルの家にまで普及したのはずっとあとの時代のことでしょう。

初めのころの仏壇は、石や土、木などで作られていたようですが、寺院や公家が作ったわけですから、豪華なものだったと思われます。

仏教が庶民のものになった現在、仏壇は仏像や経典を安置する場所であるとともに、位牌を置いて先祖の霊を祀る場ともなりました。

than he is, so the passage through this realm is not an easy one.

When this custom was transmitted from India to China, three dates were added: one hundred days, one year and three years. These may be seen as opportunities for a retrial.

Therefore in China there were ten ceremonies, but when Buddhism reached Japan, ceremonies were added for the seventh, thirteenth and thirty-third anniversaries and there were then thirteen ceremonies, and that has continued to the present day.

Q: When did Buddhist altars come to be placed in homes?

Shops selling Buddhist altar fittings take March twenty-seventh as Buddhist Altar Day, and for a reason.

According to the *Nihon Shoki*, Japan's oldest formal history, the Emperor Tenmu issued a proclamation that in the homes of the nobility throughout the land there should be built "Buddha halls" for the enshrinement of Buddhist statues and sutras. The edict was issued on March 27 in the year 686.

Therefore, the first Buddhist altars were in the temples and homes of the nobility, and it was much later that the custom extended to the general populace.

It appears that the early altars were made of stone, earth or wood, but because they were made by temples and noble families they must have been rather grand.

Now that Buddhism has become a religion of the people, in addition to being a place for statues and sutras, the Buddhist altar has become a place for installing memorial tablets and worshipping the souls of the departed.

日常の礼拝の対象となるので、信仰を持続するうえできわめて重要な存在となっています。

Q: 位牌とはなんですか？

死者の名を記し、仏壇に安置する板です。仏教では、仏壇は本尊仏や経典を祀る場としていましたが、これに儒教の考え方が混入して、仏壇に本尊仏といっしょに、故人の位牌を安置するようになったのです。

位牌は、もともとは中国で儒教の風習として用いられたもののようです。2〜3世紀ころから、10センチないし40センチくらいの板に官位や名前などを書いて、神霊に守護を願った習慣を仏教が取り入れたのです。

日本へは禅宗とともに伝わり、我が国の祖先崇拝の風潮とよくなじんで、江戸時代に一般化したと言われています。

大きさや形はいろいろで、人が亡くなった時に白木のものを作り、あとで黒や朱、金箔などで塗ったものと取り代える例が多いようです。表には戒名（または法名・法号）と亡くなった日、裏には俗名や亡くなった時の年齢などを書き記すのが一般的です。

Q: 戒名（法名・法号）とはなんですか？

私たちが浄土へ往生しても、すぐに仏になれるわけではありません。その浄土を管轄する仏の弟子になり、教えを聞いて修行をするのです。つまり、私たちが成仏するためには、一

Because the altar becomes the object of worship, it has become a very significant factor in the maintenance of faith.

Q: What is a memorial tablet?

It is a tablet on which is inscribed the name of the deceased and which is enshrined in the altar. In Buddhism, the altar was once a place for venerating figures of the Buddha or sutras, but under the influence of Confucianism, it became a place to install mortuary tablets of the deceased as well as Buddhist figures.

It appears that these tablets were originally a Confucian custom in China. Beginning in the second or third century, Buddhism adopted the custom of writing, for example, the person's name and official rank on a ten- to forty-centimeter tablet and praying to the soul of the dead person for protection.

This was introduced to Japan along with Zen Buddhism, and being similar to the trend of ancestor worship in Japan, it came into common practice in the Edo period.

The tablets come in many sizes and shapes, and there are many instances in which one is made of plain wood at the time a person dies and is later painted black or vermilion or covered with gold leaf. On the front is written the person's posthumous name given by a priest and the day the person died, and on the back is often written such things as the person's secular name and the age he or she was at death.

Q: What is the Buddhist name that is posthumously given?

Even if one is born and lives in the Pure Land, it does not mean one suddenly becomes a buddha. One becomes a disciple of the buddhas who have jurisdiction over the Pure Land, listening to the teachings and practicing. In other words, in

度、仏の弟子にならなければならないわけで
す。しかし、俗世間で汗を流して働いている私
たちが、そう簡単に出家して仏の弟子になるわ
けにはいきません。

　それで一般の人は、亡くなったあとで出家し
たことにするのです。

　出家するためには、教団の規則を守ることを
誓う「授戒」が必要です。そして授戒すると、
仏の弟子としての名前を授かります。これが
「戒名」です。戒名をもらうということは、仏
の弟子になったことを意味するのです。

　ところで親鸞聖人は、私たちは衆生を救い取
ってくれる阿弥陀仏に「南無阿弥陀仏」と報恩
感謝の念仏をすればいいのであり、戒律はいら
ないとしました。だから浄土真宗では戒名とい
わず、「法名」と言います。

　また、日蓮宗でも「南無妙法蓮華経」と唱え
ることが大事なので戒律は不要として、戒名と
いわずに「法号」と呼んでいます。

Q: 不祝儀袋の「御霊前」と「御仏前」はどう使い分けれ ばいいのですか?

　定説はないようですが、1つの考え方を紹介
しましょう。

　人は死ぬと中陰の世界に入り、死出の旅路に
つきます。そして7日ごとの裁判を受け、生前
の罪が審査されます。最後の7回目の裁判、つ
まり四十九日目に最終の判決が下り、私たちは
六道世界のいずれかか、仏の迎える浄土へ赴く
のです。

　仏たちは一様に、私たち衆生を自分の浄土に

order for us to become buddhas, we have once to become disciples of the buddha. However, those who labor in the secular world cannot so easily renounce the world and become followers of the Buddha.

Therefore, ordinary people are considered to have renounced the world when they die.

In order to become a priest, it is necessary to pledge to obey the regulations of the order and this is called "receiving the precepts." By vowing to honor the precepts, one receives a name as a follower of the Buddha. This is the *kaimyō*, or a posthumous Buddhist name. Taking this name means one has become a disciple of the Buddha.

Shinran, however, held that it was sufficient to intone the *nembutsu* of gratitude, "*Namu Amida Butsu*," to Amida who has vowed to save all sentient beings and that the precepts were unnecessary. That is why in the Jōdo Shin sect it is not called a posthumous Buddhist name but "Buddhist name."

The Nichiren sect emphasizes the chanting of "*Namu Myōhō Renge Kyō*," making the posthumous Buddhist name unnecessary and instead using the term "treasure-name."

Q: **What is the difference between *Goreizen* and *Gobu tsuzen* on the *Bushūgi-bukuro*?**

There is no definitive explanation, but let us introduce one theory.

When a person dies, he enters the realm between worlds and begins a journey to the next world. Every seven days the person undergoes a trial and an investigation of the sins committed during his or her life. At the seventh trial, that is, the forty-ninth day, the final verdict is handed down, and the person proceeds either to the world of the six realms or to the Pure Land where the Buddha awaits.

The buddhas have all taken a vow to save all sentient

救い上げる誓いを立てています。特に阿弥陀仏
などは、「南無阿弥陀仏」と称えた人はすべて
極楽浄土に救い取る、と誓願を立てています。
だから、私たちはよほどのことがないかぎり、
仏たちの浄土に往生して修行し、成仏する可能
性が高いことになります。

そこで、死者が中陰の世界をさまよっている
四十九日までは霊的な存在といえますから不祝
儀袋は「御霊前」とし、仏の道を歩んでいるそ
の後は「御仏前」とすると考えることができま
す。

もちろん、浄土へ往生するのは四十九日を経
ず、即座に行くとも考えられますから、「御霊
前」「御仏前」の違いはそんなに厳密に区別し
なくてもいいのではないでしょうか。

Q: 霊のたたりは本当にあるのですか?

あり得ません。人は死ぬと浄土へ往生する
か、四十九日以降、別の存在に生まれ変わりま
す。もし霊的な時期があるとしたら、中陰を旅
している四十九日の間でしょう。でも、この間
の死者は7日ごとに生前の罪を裁かれる被告で
すから、生きている人にたたっている余裕など
ありません。第一、被告の身で人にたたってな
どいたら、裁判官の心証を悪くするのは間違い
ありません。だから、霊がたたるなどというこ
とはないと考えていいでしょう。

仏教で死後の世界が設定されたのも、釈迦が
亡くなってからずっとあとのことで、釈迦自身
は死後のことを問われた時、「ノーコメント」
と答えました。そんなことよりも、今をいかに

beings and bring them into the Pure Land. Amida Buddha in particular has made a pledge to save and bring into the Paradise of the Pure Land everyone who intones the praise "*Namu Amida Butsu.*" Therefore, unless there are exceptional circumstances, there is a large probability that if we are reborn in the Pure Land and carry out practices there, we will become buddhas.

Therefore, because the departed is a spiritual entity during those forty-nine days following death in the interim realm, one would use "*Goreizen.*" After the departed is reborn in the Pure Land, one would use "*Gobutsuzen.*"

Of course, it may not require forty-nine days to be reincarnated in the Pure Land and the departed may go immediately, so it may not be essential to make a clear distinction between "*Goreizen*" and "*Gobutsuzen*" anyway.

Q: Is there really such a thing as being cursed by a spirit?

No. When a person dies, he is either reborn in the Pure Land or after forty-nine days is reborn in a separate existence. If there were a period of being a spirit, it would have to be these forty-nine days. However, since every seven days the person stands as a defendant for the crimes he committed during his lifetime, he would have no opportunity to seek vengeance on the living. For one thing, if a defendant were to inflict a calamity on someone, that would certainly create an unfavorable impression on the judges. It is therefore safe to assume that there is no such thing as vengeance from beyond the grave.

The world after death was constructed within Buddhism long after the Buddha's death, and when he himself was asked about what happened following death, he made no comment. He taught that rather than being concerned about such matters

生きるかが大事なのだと教えたのです。

釈迦はさらに、「無我」を説きました。永遠不変の自己などというものはない、すべては変化し、生滅するということです。ということは、仏教の開祖である釈迦も霊のたたりなどということは一言もいっていないわけです。霊のたたりは単なる迷信と思っていいでしょう。

Q: 水子地蔵とはなんですか？

人は死んで7日目に、まず秦広王の裁きを受けます。そして2番目に初江王の法廷に出向くのですが、その途中に大きな川があります。「三途の川」と呼ばれる川です。

その手前を見ると、大勢の子供たちがいる河原があります。これが有名な「賽の河原」です。子供たちは懸命に石を積み上げています。仏塔を作って仏の慈悲を受けようとしているのです。

そこに突然、鬼がやって来ました。そして、乱暴にも子供たちが積み上げた石を蹴散らし、鉄棒で子供たちを打ち据えます。子供たちは、罰を受けているのです。

子供たちになんの罪があるというのでしょうか。実は仏教では、親より先に死ぬ子供の罪は重いとされているのです。なぜならば、これほど親を悲しませることはないからです。そうはいっても、好きで死んだわけでもないのに、不憫なのは子供たちです。

地蔵
Jizō

しかし、だいじょうぶです。そこに地蔵菩薩——お地蔵さんがやって来ました。子供たちは、お地蔵さんに助けてもらえるのです。

このような伝承があるため、子供を亡くした人々は子供を水子と呼んで供養し、お地蔵さん

it was more important to consider how to live right now.

The Buddha also preached "non-self." There is no such thing as a self which remains eternally unchanged, because everything changes and appears and disappears. Hence even the Buddha, founder of the faith, said not one word concerning such things as retribution by spirits. Belief in spells and curses is simply superstition.

Q: What is a *Mizuko Jizō*?

On the seventh day after death, one is brought to trial before Shinkōō. Then one proceeds to the second court of Shokōō but along the way is a great river, called *Sanzu no Kawa*, River of Three Crossings.

There are large numbers of children along the bank known as the River-Beach of Sai. The children are desperately piling up stones. They are making a Buddhist monument in order to receive the Buddha's compassion.

Suddenly a demon comes forth, roughly scattering the stones that the children have piled up and striking the children with an iron club. The children are receiving punishment.

Why is it that they are being punished? Actually, in Buddhism it is considered a grave sin for a child to die before its parents. The reason is that there is no greater sadness for a parent than this. Having said this, it is the children who are to be pitied, for they did not die of their own accord.

Yet one need not worry, for this is where the bodhisattva Jizō comes in. *O-Jizō-san* will help the children.

Because of this tradition, people who have lost children call the children *mizu-ko*, literally "water-children," and offer

に子供の救いをお願いします。これが「水子地
蔵」の由来です

Q: 精進料理とはなんですか？

　　肉を使わない野菜料理のことです。「精進」
とは仏教の重要な徳目の1つで、修行に努め励
むことをいいます。釈迦の教えでは、煩悩をコ
ントロールするための修行である「八正道」の
1つにあげられています。
　　また、大乗仏教では「六波羅蜜」という6つ
の実践修行の目的を設定していますが、精進は
この4番目にもあげられています。
　　ところで、釈迦の時代は、必ずしも肉食は禁
じられてはいませんでした。自分のために殺す
ところを見ない肉、自分のために殺したと聞か
ない肉、自分のために殺したという疑いのない
肉は食べてもよかったのです。
　　ところが、大乗仏教の時代になると、不殺生
の考えと強く結びついたのでしょうか、肉食が
禁じられます。ヒンドゥー教からの影響も大き
かったようです。いずれにしても、大乗仏教で
は僧は肉食をやめ、ベジタリアンとなります。

　　日本も大乗仏教ですから、この戒律は守られ
ました。そして、日頃は肉や魚を食べている在
家の仏教徒も、先祖の命日や忌日には肉食を避
け、野菜を食べて「精進日」としました。そん
なところから菜食と精進が結びつき、精進料理
と呼ばれるものが誕生することになったと思わ
れます。

prayers for them, asking Jizō to save them. This is the origin of *Mizuko-Jizō*.

Q: What is *shōjin ryōri*?

Essentially this is vegetarian meals without meat. *Shōjin*, meaning assiduity, is considered one of the significant virtues in Buddhism, and it means to devotedly endeavor to practice. In the Buddha's teachings, it is included in the Eightfold Noble Path which is the practice carried out to remove illusions.

Within Mahayanist Buddhism, six goals are established for actual practice in order to attain buddhahood, and shōjin is listed as number four.

At the time the Buddha lived, it was not absolutely prohibited to eat meat. It was acceptable to eat meat which one had not seen slaughtered for oneself, not being informed that it was slaughtered for oneself, and which one did not think might have been slaughtered for oneself.

However, with the rise of Mahayana thought, possibly because it became tied with abstinence from taking life, the eating of meat came to be prohibited. It seems that the influence of Hinduism was considerable. Whatever the case, Mahayanist thought decrees that priests are forbidden to eat meat and must become vegetarians.

Japanese Buddhism is Mahayanist, so this rule was obeyed. Even laypersons, whose everyday diet included meat and fish, avoided eating meat on days commemorating the Buddha's birth and death, by eating vegetables only on these "vegetarian days." From this the eating of a vegetarian diet and assiduity became tied and it is assumed that this is the origin of *shōjin ryōri*.

Q: 死者はなぜ北枕で寝るのですか?

　　釈迦は80歳の時、故郷のカピラヴァスツに向けて旅をしました。しかし、途中クシナガラというところまで来た時、信者の施した食べ物にあたって病気になってしまいました。

　　釈迦はシャーラ樹の林に横たわり、侍者のアーナンダの介護を受けましたが、そのかいなく亡くなってしまいます。

　　釈迦は息を引き取る時、右脇を下にし、頭を北に向け、顔を西に面して亡くなったといいます。このことにちなんで、死者を北枕に寝かせるのです。

　　釈迦が亡くなったときに、シャーラ樹の葉が真っ白に変色したといわれ、それで、今でも祭壇のいちばん上には白い花を一対飾るのだそうです。

Q: 坐禅はどうすればいいのですか?

　　坐禅は釈迦が悟りを開いた時の方法です。「禅」とは古代インドの「ディヤーナ」という言葉の音写で、心の乱れを防いで精神を統一することをいいます。瞑想といってもいいでしょう。ですから、坐禅は、基本的に、坐って精神を統一すればいいのです。

　　坐り方にはいろいろな方法があります。釈迦が悟りを開いた時は「結跏趺坐」という坐り方をしていたといいます。「結跏」とは足を組むこと、「趺坐」とは足の裏を見せて坐ることだといいます。次のようにして行います。

　　まず、座布団(正式には坐蒲)を二つ折りにしてお尻の下に敷きます。足には敷きません。そして右の足を左のもものつけねに乗せ、次い

Q: Why are the dead placed with the pillow to the north?

When the Buddha was eighty years old, he made a journey to his homeland Kapilavastu. Along the route at Kusinaga, he fell ill after eating something prepared by a believer.

The Buddha lay down in a grove of sala trees and was treated by his companion Ananda, but the treatment was ineffectual and he died.

It is said that when he breathed his last the Buddha was lying on his right side, with his pillow to the north and facing west. It is in connection with this that the deceased are placed with the head to the north.

It is also said that when the Buddha died, the leaves of the sala grove changed color and became white. This is said to be the reason why even now white flowers are placed opposite one another at the top of the Buddhist altar.

Q: What is the proper way to do seated meditation?

Seated meditation, *zazen*, is the posture of the Buddha when he achieved enlightenment. "*Zen*" is a transliteration of the Indian word *dhyana*, meaning concentrating the spirit and staving off disturbances of the mind. It may also be called contemplation. So in order to do *zazen*, fundamentally one need only sit and focus one's mind.

There are various ways to sit. At his awakening, the Buddha sat cross-legged in the posture called *kekka-fuza*. One sits with one's legs bent crossways under the body, showing the soles of the feet. It is done as follows.

First, a sitting cushion is folded in two and placed under the buttocks, not under the legs. Place the right foot on top of the left thigh and the left foot on top of the right thigh.

座禅
Seated meditation

で左足を右もものつけねに乗せます。

　次に右手の手のひらを上にして組んだ足の上に乗せます。その上に左手の手のひらを重ね、両手の親指を軽くつけて輪を作ります。

　へその下5～6センチのところを前に突き出し、重心をすべて腰にかけます。そして背骨をまっすぐに伸ばせば形はでき上がりです。

　息はゆっくりと十分に吐き出し、その反動で酸素が入ってくるように吸い込みます。そして雑念を払い、精神を統一するのです。

　口では簡単に言っても、そうやすやすと雑念を払えるものではありません。禅道場で、専門家の指導を受けることをお勧めします。

Q: 除夜の鐘は、なぜ108回ならすのですか？

　一般に、煩悩の数が108あるといわれており、これを取り除くことを願って、年末の夜半に寺で梵鐘が108回打たれるのです。

　インドでは108という数が重要視され、聖なる言葉を念じるのに108回行ったり、数珠の珠の数を108個にしたり、法門や煩悩の数を108にしたりしたようです。

　これが中国に伝わり、寺院で朝と夕、108回、鐘を突くようになったといわれます。後には18回に省略されますが、朝は目を覚ますために、夕は迷いを覚ますために打たれたといいます。

　さらに日本に伝わると、この風習は年末の行事となりました。1年を通じて身にこびりついた欲望や執着を捨て、清浄な気持ちで新年を迎えようという習慣となって定着したのです。

Next, place the right hand palm up on top of the crossed legs. On top of it place the left hand on top of the palm so that the thumbs touch lightly forming a circle.

Extend forward the portion of the body five or six centimeters below the navel, placing one's center of gravity in the pelvic region. Extend the spine and the posture is complete.

Breathe out slowly and completely, and breathe in so that oxygen comes in by counteraction. Clear away random thoughts and concentrate the mind.

It sounds easy, but it is not so easy to banish worldly concerns from the mind. It is recommended to receive instruction from a specialist at a Zen practice hall.

Q: Why is the bell struck 108 times at "*Joya no kane*"?

It is generally said that there are 108 earthly passions, and that the bells at Buddhist temples are rung beginning at midnight on New Year's Eve with the hope of dispelling these passions.

The number 108 was considered significant in India, such that sacred words were chanted 108 times, 108 beads were strung in a rosary, and there were held to be 108 teachings and 108 passions.

When Buddhism was introduced to China, the bells at temples were struck 108 times both morning and evening. This was later reduced to eighteen times, but it was done each morning to awaken one from sleep and each evening to awaken one from illusions.

In Japan this became a year-end year-beginning custom. It became established as a custom to cast aside the desires and attachments that had stuck to oneself during the year and to greet the new year with a feeling of purity.

Q:「お盆」の意味を教えてください。

「盂蘭盆会」を略して「お盆」といっているのです。盂蘭盆とは「ウランバナ」という古代インドの言葉の音写で、逆さ吊りの苦しみという意味を表します。

釈迦の弟子に、もっとも神通力に秀でたマウドガルヤーヤナという人がいました。日本では「目連」という名で知られています。この目連が、死んだ母のその後のようすを神通力で見てみると、母は餓鬼道に落ちて苦しんでいました。なにかを食べようとすると、すべて火となって食べられないのです。

目連は母の逆さ吊りにされたような苦しみを見てショックを受け、釈迦に相談しました。すると釈迦は、僧たちの雨期の修行期間が明けた7月15日に、僧たちに食べ物などを布施してお母さんの幸せを祈りなさいと教えました。

この故事にのっとり、先祖を供養する盂蘭盆会が7月15日に行われるようになったといいますが、我が国ではもっと古くからあった祖霊信仰の習俗と混交し、独特の風習となったようです。

日本で最初に行われたお盆は、606年7月15日、推古天皇の時といわれています。先祖の魂を信じて大事にしてきた日本人の心情によくなじみ、盂蘭盆会は日本流の形で定着したのでしょう。

Q:「お彼岸」の意味を教えてください。

「彼岸」のことで、日本独特の行事といわれています。春分の日と秋分の日のそれぞれをはさんだ前後3日間、各7日をいい、お寺では読経

Q: What is the meaning of *O-bon*?

O-bon is an abbreviation of *Urabon-e*, which is a translit-eration of the Indian word *ullambana*, a word which denotes the suffering that comes from being hung upside down.

Among the Buddha's disciples, there was one named Maudgalyayana who possessed exceptional divine powers. In Japan he is known as Mokuren. By means of his divine powers he sought to see what was happening to his mother after her death, only to find she had fallen into and was suffering in the hell of hungry spirits. Whatever she tried to eat turned into fire and could not be eaten.

Mokuren was shocked at seeing his mother suffering as much as if she had been hung upside down and he sought the counsel of the Buddha. The Buddha then taught his disciples to donate food and pray for their mothers' happiness on July 15, the day that their rainy season practices came to an end.

From this event, *ullambana* which venerates one's ances-tors came to be carried out on July 15. In Japan this merged with the folk custom of ancestor worship which had its origin in the most ancient times and became a unique custom.

The first *O-bon* was said to have been observed on July 15 in the year 606 during the time of the Empress Suiko. Proba-bly because it suited the feelings of the Japanese people who had believed in and venerated the souls of their ancestors, *urabon-e* became established in this Japanese form.

Q: What is the meaning of *O-higan*?

It refers to *Higan-e*, a unique Japanese observance. This is the seven-day period, the vernal or autumnal equinox plus the three days before and after, in which temples hold Buddhist

墓参り
Visit to a grave

や法話などをして法要を行い、信者はお寺やお墓をお参りします。

　お彼岸の起源は古く、聖徳太子のころから行われているともいわれています。

　彼岸とは「此岸」に対する言葉です。此岸は苦しみに満ちたこの世で、彼岸は理想の浄土を意味します。此岸にいる人は、特にこの7日間、仏道に励んで彼岸に渡る努力をしようというわけです。自分の悟りを求め、また亡くなった先祖を供養するのです。

　この場合の仏道とは、大乗仏教の修行徳目である「六波羅蜜」を実践することと考えられます。六波羅蜜の波羅蜜とは、古代インドの「パーラミター」という言葉の音写で、パーラミターとは「到彼岸」、つまり彼岸に渡るという意味だからです。六波羅蜜とは次の6つです。

　（1）布施……欲を捨て、大事なものを仏や苦しむ人たちに施すこと。
　（2）持戒……戒律を守ること。
　（3）忍辱……はずかしめに耐え忍び、怒りにとらわれないこと。
　（4）精進……善に向けて努め励むこと。
　（5）禅定……心を落ちつかせて精神統一すること。
　（6）智慧……真実を見る目を持つこと。

　せめてお彼岸の期間だけでも、このような心がけで過ごしたいものです。

Q：「花祭り」の意味を教えてください。

　釈迦の誕生を祝う行事で、灌仏会ともいわれます。「灌」とは頭上に水を注ぐことで、インドの国王即位式などの時に灌頂と呼ばれて行われていました。4月8日、これにちなんで、誕

services such as the reading of sutras and lectures and believers pay visits to temples and graves.

The origin of *O-higan* is ancient and is thought to date back to the time of Prince Shōtoku.

Higan, "that shore," is opposed to *shigan*, "this shore." *Shigan* is this world full of suffering; *higan* is the ideal Pure Land. Those who are on "this shore" make special efforts in this seven-day period to follow the path of the Buddha and reach the "other shore." One pursues one's own enlightenment and venerates one's dead ancestors.

In this case, the path of the Buddha can be taken as practicing the Six Perfections, the six kinds of practice of Mahayana Buddhism. The word *haramitsu* in *rokuharamitsu* comes from the Indian word *paramita*, meaning "reaching the other shore." The Six Perfections are as follows:

(1) *fuse* —- casting aside desire and donating something significant for the buddha or those who are suffering
(2) *jikai* —- keeping the precepts
(3) *ninniku* —- perseverance in enduring insults and not being swept away by passion
(4) *shōjin*—- assiduously endeavoring toward doing good
(5) *zenjō* —- calming the mind and concentrating the spirit

(6) *chie* —- having eyes to see actual truth
One wants to endeavor in these practices especially during these periods called *O-higan*.

Q: Please explain the meaning of *Hana Matsuri*.

This is an observance to celebrate the birth of the Buddha and it is also known as *kambutsu-e*. "*Kan*" means to sprinkle water on the head, and it was carried out in India as part of an enthronement ceremony for kings. The observation on April

天地を指した
釈迦の像
Figure of
Budda pointing
to heaven and
earth

生した仏の像の頭に甘茶や水などをかけ、釈迦の誕生を祝います。

　釈迦の母のマーヤー夫人は、出産のために里帰りする途中、ルンビニー苑に立ち寄りました。そして木に右手を差しかけた時、右脇から釈迦が生まれ出ました。生まれた釈迦はその場で立ち上がり、右手で天を指し、左手で地を指して7歩あゆみ、「天上天下唯我独尊」と言ったと伝えられています。

　この姿を模した天地を指す仏の像は、花で飾られた堂の中央に安置されます。その像に水や甘茶をかけ、仏の誕生を祝うのが花祭りです。

　我が国では606年、元興寺で行われたことが『日本書紀』に載っています。江戸時代に非常に盛んになり、甘茶が用いられるようになったのもこの時代以降のことのようです。

eighth celebrates the birth of the Buddha by sprinkling sweet tea or water on the head of Buddhist images.

On her way home to give birth, Queen Maya stopped in the Lumbini Garden. When she put out her right hand to touch a tree, the Buddha was born from her right side. At the moment of birth, the Buddha is said to have immediately stood up, right hand toward heaven and left hand toward earth, taken seven steps and proclaimed, "I alone am honored, in heaven and on earth."

A figure showing the Buddha pointing to heaven and earth is placed in the center of the hall. The sprinkling of water or sweet tea upon this statue to celebrate the birth of the Buddha is *Hana Matsuri*.

It is recorded in the *Nihon Shoki* that this was observed at Gangōji in 606. It became quite popular in the Edo period and it was from about that time that sweet tea, *amacha*, came to be used.

8

仏教と神道、キリスト教

Buddhism, Shintō and Christianity

Q: 仏教と神道の根本的な違いはどこにありますか？

　　仏教には釈迦という開祖がおり、無常や無
我、四諦や八正道、また、縁起の思想などの教
理があります。ところが神道には教祖といわれ
る人はいませんし、教理というものもありませ
ん。そこがもっとも大きな違いといえるでしょ
う。

　　古代の日本人は、この世に存在するいっさい
の物事に神が宿っているとして、その多くの
神々を崇拝してきました。しかし、神自体はそ
の姿を見せず、神霊はなにかの姿を借りて現

Q: What are the fundamental differences between Buddhism and Shintoism?

Buddhism has a founder called the Buddha, and doctrines such as "impermanence" and "non-self," the Four Noble Truths, the Eightfold Noble Path, and the concept of causation. In contrast, Shintoism has no one who could be called a founder and has no doctrines. This is surely the major difference between the two.

Ancient Japanese believed that deities reside in everything in this world and they worshipped these numerous deities. While the deities do not show themselves directly, the divine spirit borrows some form and communicates with humans.

れ、人間と交信します。ですから、山や森、木々の一つ一つ、川や海など、あらゆるものの中に神は存在しているのです。

とにかくたくさんの神がいるわけですから、その神の中には、人々を守ったりする神もいれば、たたりをもたらしたりする神もいます。それが神道であり、日本固有の民族宗教です。

それに対して、仏教は釈迦の説いた哲学であり、その教理には民族を超えた普遍性があります。そのため仏教は国境を越え、東南アジアや中国、朝鮮半島や日本などにも伝わったのです。

このように教祖がいて、教理があり、その教理には普遍性があって世界に広まった宗教を、世界宗教と呼んでいます。仏教やキリスト教、イスラム教などがそうです。仏教と神道には、世界宗教と民族宗教の違いがあるのです。

Q: お経と祝詞はどう違いますか？

お経は釈迦の教えを整理し、編纂したもので、具体的なたとえ話や論理を駆使して構成されています。時代が下るにつれて呪術的な色彩が多くつけ加えられましたが、その内容はあくまで人間の生き方や世界の構造を説いた教理です。つまり、お経は人々を真理に導くため、仏から人々に発せられた言葉であると言うことができます。

それに対して祝詞は、神と人間の交信に使われる言葉だと言うことができます。本居宣長という学者は、祝詞は人間から神に申し上げる言葉であるといい、折口信夫という学者は、神が人間に下す命令である、と主張しました。

Therefore, in each and every mountain, forest, tree, river and sea, there exists a deity.

There are innumerable deities, and among them are some who protect human beings and others who wreak vengeance upon humans. This is Shintoism, a particularly Japanese folk religion.

In contrast, Buddhism is a philosophy preached by the Buddha and its doctrines have a universality that transcends a particular ethnic group. It is for this reason that Buddhism crossed national borders and was transmitted to Southeast Asia, China, the Korean Peninsula and Japan.

We call a faith that has a founder, doctrines and a universality in its teachings which spread across the world a "world religion." Buddhism, along with Christianity and Islam, fits this category, and this is another difference with Shintoism, which is a folk religion.

Q: What is the difference between sutras and *norito*?

Sutras are the teachings of the Buddha which have been arranged and edited and are organized in such a way that they make use of concrete examples and logic. Through periods of history, many elements of incantation came to be added to them, but in the content remained the teachings which preached the way human beings should live and the structure of the world. In sum, the scriptures lead people toward truth and it can be said that they are the words of the Buddha uttered to human beings.

In contrast, Shintō *norito* can be seen as incantations through which deities and humans communicate. The scholar Motoori Norinaga said that *norito* were sacred incantations by which human beings addressed the gods. Another scholar, Origuchi Shinobu, stressed that they were commands which

　　日本人は古代から言葉には霊力が込められているとして、言葉を「言霊」と呼んで崇めてきました。祝詞はまさにこの言霊の代表なのです。だから罪の穢れを祓う時や、お祭り、地鎮祭、結婚式、初宮詣などのおり、その霊力を頼んで祝詞を唱えるのです。

　　仏教にも「陀羅尼」といって、仏の教えが封じ込められていて、すべてのことを心に記憶して忘れない力、または修行者を守護する力を持つという章句がありますが、祝詞はこれと似ているところがあるかもしれません。

Q: 僧侶と神主はどう違うのですか？

　　僧侶というのは、釈迦の教えを実践し、人々に伝える仏弟子たちです。釈迦の教えとは、苦である現実とその原因を知り、それを取り除く修行をして安楽の境地を得ることです。そして、他の人々を同じ境地に導くことです。その教えの実現のために、出家して、寺に住み、修行をしているのが僧です。

　　自らの修行とともに、僧は、葬儀などの法事に関することを執り行いますが、僧であるということは、まず第一に、僧自身が悟りを開くための道なのです。

　　この点が神主と根本的に違っていて、神主であるということは、神主自身の自己実現の道ではなく、超常的な神の言葉を聞き、その言葉を人々に伝え、また、人々の声を神に伝えるというのが基本的な役目です。日常は、神が霊を宿

the gods issued to human beings.

From ancient times, Japanese have held that language possesses spiritual power, and they have worshipped this as the "soul of language." The *norito* are truly representative of this spirit within words. Therefore, at times of purification or defilement and at festivals, ground-breaking ceremonies, weddings and first visits to a shrine of a newborn, these sacred incantations are intoned in order to invoke this sacred power.

Buddhism also has *dharani*, mystic syllables which are held to possess the teachings of the Buddha, the power to remember whatever is committed to memory, and the power to protect the practitioner. In some ways, they are similar to the Shintō *norito*.

Q: What is the difference between Buddhist priests and Shinto priests?

Buddhist priests are followers of the Buddha who practice the teachings of the Buddha and transmit them to other people. What the Buddha teaches is to recognize the actual truth of suffering and its causes and to achieve a state of bliss by practicing to eliminate its causes. Priests are also supposed to lead others to this same stage. In order to manifest these teachings, the priests take religious orders, live in a temple and carry out various practices.

While continuing his own practices, the priest also performs Buddhist services such as funerals, but being a priest means first and foremost following the path toward reaching one's own enlightenment.

This is fundamentally different from the Shintō priest, for being a priest is not a path to self-realization. The priest's fundamental role is to listen to the supernatural words of the gods and communicate them to human beings, as well as fulfilling the role of communicating the voice of the people to the gods.

す施設である神社を守り、神事に関することを司りますが、あくまで、人々や共同体と神との仲介役をするのが神主です。

　神は穢れを嫌い、天変地異などを通じて、人々や共同体に災いをもたらすことがあります。そんな時、なんとかして神に鎮まってもらわなければなりません。そのためには、神に願いを聞き届けてもらわなければなりません。また、なんらかの方法で神の声に耳を傾けなければなりません。そんな時に、神と人々や共同体との仲立ちをするのが神主といえるでしょう。

Q:合掌と柏手の違いはどんなところにありますか?

　合掌とは、左右の手のひらを胸の前で合わせることです。これは必ずしも神仏に対する行為とは限らず、古代からインドや東南アジアなどで一般のあいさつに用いられている作法だといいます。相手を敬いますという表現です。

　インドでは右手を浄、左手を不浄として使い分けていますが、その両手を合わせるということには、トータルな真実の自己を表すという意味があります。この作法が仏教に取り入れられ、仏を信じて従いますという気持ちを表す動作として、今日まで続いているというわけです。

　一方、柏手とは、神前に向かって手を打ち鳴らすことです。これは、日本古来の歴史書である『古事記』や『日本書紀』にある「天地開闢」、つまり、混沌としていた天地が2つに分かれて、日本が誕生した時の音、または、岩屋に閉じこもった天照大御神を引き出す時の、天の岩戸をこじ開けた時の音を模しているとい

Ordinarily, the Shintō priest's duty is to take care of the shrine facilities where the spirit of the deity resides and to perform Shintō rites. In a strict sense, the Shintō priest is an intermediary between the people or community and the gods.

The gods dislike impurities and by means of natural calamities bring forth misfortunes on people and communities. At such times, it becomes necessary to appease the deity in some fashion. To do this requires communicating the request to the gods. At the same time, one has to turn one's ears to the voice of the god. At such times, it is the Shintō priest who performs the role of intermediary between the people or community and the deity.

Q: What is the difference between *gasshō* and *kashiwade*?

Gasshō is putting the palms of one's hands together in front of one's chest. This is not limited to acts vis-a-vis the gods and buddhas, but is said to have been a form of general greeting in India and Southeast Asia from ancient times. It is an expression of respect for the other person.

In India the right hand is considered pure and the left hand is considered impure, and the placing of the two hands together represents the total, true self. Buddhism adopted this form of decorum and has up to the present day used it to indicate the belief in and desire to obey the Buddha.

Kashiwade is clapping the hands together before a deity. This is the sound which according to the story of the creation of heaven and earth recorded in Japan's ancient *Kojiki* and *Nihon Shoki* divided the chaos into heaven and earth and gave birth to Japan. It is also said to be patterned on the sound of the closing of the door of the cave after Amaterasu had come out of the cave where she had sequestered herself. Whichever the

われています。どちらにしても、光が輝き出す
ことを祈念しての行為なのでしょう。

　合掌と柏手の由来は違いますが、胸の前で手
を合わせる宗教行為だということでは共通して
います。キリスト教やほかの宗教でも、同じよ
うに胸の前で手を合わせます。人間が人間を超
えた存在に対する時、思わず行ってしまう共通
の動作なのでしょうか。たいへん興味深いこと
だと思います。

Q: 神道には女神がいるのに、なぜ菩薩は男ばかりなのですか？

　もしかすると、性差別が存在するのかもしれ
ません。もちろん古代の話ですが、日本は母系
制社会といわれるように、神話などではむしろ
女性が重要視されています。

　それに対して仏教の発祥地であるインドで
は、女性の地位を低く見る傾向があったようで
す。

　神道のテキストともなっている歴史書、『古
事記』『日本書紀』によると、この日本列島を
作った伊邪那岐と伊邪那美という夫婦の３人の
子供のうち、女性である天照大御神が最上の
世界である天の高天原を支配します。これは女
性上位の扱いといえるでしょう。

　一方、インドでは女性の身では仏や世界を支
配する転輪聖王にはなれないとされていまし
た。女性は善行をなし、一度男性に生まれ変わ
ってからでないと聖なる存在にはなれないと考
えられていたのです。そのため、仏の一歩前の
段階にいる菩薩には男性が多いのです。そこに
は女性差別の視点があったのかもしれません。

case, it is an act of prayer in hopes that light will shine forth.

While *gassho* and *kashiwade* differ in their origins, they share in common the fact that they are religious acts that involve placing the hands in front of the chest. In Christianity and other religions believers also join their hands together in front of their chests. Could it be that this is a subconscious act on the part of human beings when they encounter an existence that exceeds humanity? This is an extremely interesting thought.

Q: Why is it that there are female deities in Shintō, but bodhisattvas are always male?

There may be a form of sexual discrimination here. Of course we are talking about ancient times, but just as it is said that Japan was a matrilineal society, in legends and such, women were looked upon as important.

In contrast, in the birthplace of Buddhism in India, the position of women tended to be inferior.

According to the histories recorded in the *Kojiki* and *Nihon Shoki*, which also serve as texts for Shintoism, of the three children of the husband and wife Izanagi and Izanami who created the Japanese Archipelago, the daughter Amaterasu Ōmikami reigned over Takamagahara, the High Celestial Plain. Surely this shows the priority given to women.

In contrast, in India it was held that women could not become a buddha or a Wheel-turning Noble King who rules the world. It was believed that to become a holy entity, a woman had to first perform good acts and be reborn as a man. For that reason, there are many men among the bodhisattvas, who are one step away from becoming buddhas. This may be a view that reflects discrimination against women.

　しかし、その後大乗仏教の経典である『法華
経』などでは、なみいる男の菩薩や僧たちの前
で、みごとに仏になってみせる女性の話が紹介
されていますから、女性に対する扱いにも歴史
的な変遷があるのでしょう。

Q: 仏教には仏像があるのに、神道には神像はないのですか？

　実は、仏教でも当初は、仏像を作ることはタ
ブーでした。釈迦は自己を灯明とし、法を灯明
としなさい、と言って亡くなったのですから、
釈迦の像を灯明とすることはできなかったので
す。
　しかし、人々は信仰の拠り所を求め、紀元後
１世紀ないし２世紀ころから、次第に仏像が作
られ、礼拝の対象となっていきました。その後
は世界各地で仏教美術が花開き、多様な仏像が
作られていったのです。それも、仏像に投影で
きる釈迦という教祖がいたからこそ可能だった
のでしょう。

　ところが、神道には教祖と言われる存在はあ
りません。それに、神に人の姿のイメージが与
えられたのは『古事記』『日本書紀』が書かれ
てからであって、それ以前の日本の神は、森羅
万象であり、自然そのものでした。だから神に
は姿がなく、偶像化できなかったのです。
　神社には鏡や剣、石などの「御神体」または
「御霊代」などと呼ばれるものがありますが、
これも神の象徴などではなく、神霊が宿る神聖
なモノなのです。ですから、本来、神像は作り
得ないものだったのですが、それでも『古事
記』『日本書紀』以後、神話のストーリーをも

However, in later scriptures such as the *Lotus Sutra* of Mahayana Buddhism, there are stories of women who are able to become buddhas before a succession of male bodhisattvas and priests, so there is a historical restitution even in the treatment of women.

Q: Why are there images of the Buddha, but no images of the gods?

Actually, in the beginning it was taboo to make figures of the Buddha. Just before he died, the Buddha told his followers, "Make the self your light, make the Law your light." As a result, one was not able to make a statue of the Buddha one's light.

However, the religious spirit of the people sought a ground for their faith and from about the first or second century they began to create Buddhist figures and make them objects of worship. Later Buddhist art blossomed in many parts of the world and many varieties of statues of the Buddha were created. Again we should note that it was because there was a historical Buddha who founded the faith that such figures came into existence.

In Shintō, on the other hand, there is no entity that could reasonably be called a founder. It was only with the writing of the *Kojiki* and the *Nihon Shoki* that the gods were given anthropomorphic qualities; before that time the gods of Japan were all creation and nature itself. Therefore, the deities had no form and could not be made into icons.

In shrines one finds mirrors, swords and stones which are called *goshintai*, objects of worship, or *mitamashiro*, things worshipped as symbols, but these are not symbols of the gods, but rather sacred objects in which the divine spirit resides. Therefore, in the beginning making images of the deities was impossible, whereas following the *Kojiki* and *Nihon Shoki*,

とにしてさまざまな神々の絵が描かれ、像が刻まれて今日に伝えられています。

Q: 仏壇と神棚が1つの家にあっても、日本ではなぜおかしくないのですか？

　　神道では、存在するすべての物事を神と見て、崇め祀りますから、日本人にとって神道は、宗教というよりも、生活そのものだったのだと思われます。農業において畑の神に豊作を祈り、漁業において海の神に豊漁を祈り、お祀りをするというようにです。

　そんな日本に入ってきた仏教は、神道とは別の新しい文化であり、哲学であり、またご利益をもたらす祈祷でもありました。それに、新しい日本を支えるモラルでもありました。だから、生活のレベルでは神のお祀りを営み、一方、文化や宗教のレベルで仏教を尊ぶことに、さほど違和感がなかったものと思われます。

　そこで神仏混交という現象が起こり、神社や寺で神と仏とがいっしょに祀られることになります。その理論的な裏づけとして考え出されたのが、平安末期から鎌倉時代にかけて盛んになった「本地垂迹説」でした。すなわち、神道の神々は、仏教の仏・菩薩たちが神々の姿を借りて現れたのだというのです。

　この考えが定着して、日本では神と仏をいっしょに祀ることがむしろ自然なこととみなされるようになっていきました。明治時代には国の方針として、神と仏を分離する政策がとられたことがありますが、神と仏を共に崇めるという習慣は、人々の間に強く残ったままです。

based upon the narratives of the myths, pictures and figures could be produced and this has continued to the present day.

Q: Why don't Japanese think it strange to have a Buddhist altar and a Shintō altar in the same house?

Shintō sees all existing things as deities and venerates them, so for Japanese, Shintō is less a religion than it is life itself. In the farming community they hold festivals to pray to the gods of the fields for rich harvests and in the fishing industry they pray to the gods of the sea for rich catches.

The Buddhism that was introduced presented them with an entirely different culture and philosophy and it also had prayers that brought benefits. It served as a new morality that could support the new nation. Therefore one can say that the Japanese felt little contradiction between carrying out festivals for the gods of everyday life and esteeming Buddhism within the realm of culture and religion.

Hence the phenomenon of syncretism occurred, with shrines and temples enshrining gods and buddhas. The theoretical support evolved for this was the "theory of original prototype and local manifestation" which flourished from the late Heian into the Kamakura period. This held that the Shintō divinities are manifestations of the buddhas and boddhisattvas of Buddhism.

This notion took root, and it came to be seen as entirely natural in Japan that gods and buddhas were enshrined together. In the Meiji period it became government policy to separate Shintō and Buddhism, but the custom of worshipping them together remains firmly entrenched among the people.

Q: 檀家と氏子とはどう違うのですか？

檀家とは、自分の信仰する特定の寺院に所属し、法事や葬儀などの仏事を執り行ってもらったりする一方、寺に布施をしてこれを支える家のことです。ですから、基本的には自分の信仰心によって寺を選ぶわけです。

それに対して、氏子は地縁や血縁によって神と結びついています。

土地の神を「産土神」といいますが、ある土地の人々は、その土地の産土神に産み出された子孫だとして、自分たちを守ってくれる神を共同でお祭りします。この場合、その土地に住む人々が、皆、氏子になるわけです。

また、春日神社における藤原氏や、梅宮神社における橘氏のように、ある氏族の「氏神」となっていて、その氏族の子孫を氏子と呼ぶ場合があります。この場合、その血縁でつながった人たちが、皆、氏子になります。

ですから、檀家が自分で寺を選ぶのに対して、氏子はもともと氏神社が決まっていることが、両者の違いの1つだと言えます。

ただ、信仰によって選ぶはずだった檀家が、江戸幕府の政策によって、住民が強制的にその土地の寺院に所属させられてしまったということがあったことを、つけ加えておかなければならないでしょう。

Q: 仏教とキリスト教の根本的な違いは？

キリスト教では、唯一絶対の神の存在を説きます。イエス・キリストはその神の子とされ、

Q: What is the difference between *danka* and *ujiko*?

Danka indicates a family that belongs to a particular temple within the faith of that family. The family requests that the temple conduct funeral and memorial services in exchange for donations to support the temple. Fundamentally, the family selects the temple out of its own religious convictions.

In contrast, *ujiko* are bound with a deity based on residence or blood relationship.

The protective deity of one's birthplace is called *ubusunagami*. This deity is held to have given birth to all the people within a particular geographic territory, and those families worship as a community the deity that protects them. In this instance, all of the people who live in that locale are called *ujiko*.

There are also instances, such as with the Fujiwara and the Kasuga Shrine or the Tachibana and the Umemiya Shrine, where the deity also becomes the *ujigami*, clan deity, and all of the descendants of that clan became *ujiko*. All those bound by blood are therefore *ujiko*.

Therefore, the fact that the *danka* choose their own temple and the clan shrine of the *ujiko* is already determined is a central difference between the two.

It should be noted that where the *danka* had made their selection of a temple according to their religious beliefs, in the Edo period as a result of the government policy of the bakufu, residents of a particular locality were forced to become members of a particular local temple.

Q: What is the fundamental difference between Buddhism and Christianity?

Christianity preaches the existence of a single absolute deity. Jesus Christ is that deity's son and God manifests Him-

神はイエス・キリストを通じて人間の心の中に
その姿を現します。

この神は、万物の創造主であり、世界の支配
者です。だからイエス・キリストは、人々に神
を信じ、その守護を受けるように教えました。
「求めよ、さらば与えられん」と説いたのです。

それに対して、仏教ではあらゆる絶対的なも
のを否定します。絶対不変の事象などはなく、
すべては変化生滅するといって「無常」を主張
し、永遠不滅の自我は存在しないといって「無
我」を説くのです。

そしてあらゆるものの存在の原理を、「縁起」
の思想で説明します。すべての物事は一定の原
因の結果としてあり、またその因を補助する縁
によって生起している。だからその因と縁が変
われば、すべても変化する相対的な存在である
としたのです。

以上のように、キリスト教では絶対的な神の
存在を主張し、仏教では絶対的なものの存在を
認めないというところが両者の根本的な違いと
いえるでしょう。

Q: 釈迦とイエス・キリストの共通点と違いはどこにあり ますか？

2人にはかなりの共通点があります。

2人とも仏教・キリスト教という世界宗教の
教祖です。そして2人は人々にそれぞれの真理
を宣べ伝え、人々を救済しようとしてその生涯
をささげました。

さらに、釈迦には人間としての側面と悟りを
開いてからの仏としての側面がありますが、イ
エス・キリストにも人間イエスの顔と救世主キ
リストとしての顔があるといわれます。そし

self in the human heart through Jesus.

This deity is the creator of all things and ruler of the universe. Jesus Christ teaches people to believe in God and accept his protection. "Ask and you shall be given," he preached.

In contrast, Buddhism denies all absolutes. It preaches that nothing is absolutely permanent and emphasizes the transformation and extinction of all things in the teaching of "impermanence" and the non-existence of a self that is eternally non-extinguishing in the teaching of "non-self."

It explains the original nature of all things in the notion of "causation." Everything is the result of a particular cause and is brought about by certain supplementary conditions. Therefore, if that cause and condition change, it makes everything relative to the change.

In this way, Christianity emphasizes the existence of an absolute divinity, but Buddhism does not recognize the existence of any absolute. This is the fundamental difference between the two.

Q: What are the similarities and dissimilarities between the Buddha and Jesus Christ?

There are a number of similarities between the two.

First, they are the respective founders of Buddhism and Christianity. They both devoted their lives to the propagation of their respective truths and to saving people.

Moreover, the Buddha has two aspects—that of a human and that of one who has attained enlightenment. This is also true of Christ, who has a human aspect and a divine aspect as the Savior Christ. The teachings of both still give encourage-

て、彼らの教えはいまだに世界中のおおぜいの
人々の心を励まし、支えているのです。

2人の違いは、まずその教えにあります。キ
リストは絶対者としての神への帰依を説いたの
に対し、釈迦は絶対という概念を否定しまし
た。

また、その伝道の方法にも違いがあったよう
です。弟子たちが伝道に行く時、キリストは2
人以上で行くように命じたのに対し、釈迦は1
人で行くように言ったといいます。釈迦の時代
は比較的安定して平和でしたが、キリストの時
代、イスラエルはローマの支配下にあり、危険
に満ちていたという事情があったようです。

2人の亡くなり方も大きく違いました。キリ
ストは捕らわれてはりつけになったのに対し、
釈迦は80歳まで生きて、生きとし生けるものの
涙に送られて亡くなったといわれています。

Q: 聖書とお経はどう違いますか?

お経は釈迦の教えを弟子たちが整理し、編纂
した仏教の聖典です。

それに対して、聖書には2種あります。『旧
約聖書』と『新約聖書』です。『旧約聖書』は
ユダヤ教の聖典でもあり、古代からの神とイス
ラエルとのかかわりを歴史的に記したもので
す。『新約聖書』はこのユダヤ教を変革したイ
エス・キリストの弟子たちがまとめたもので、
「福音書」や書簡類などからなります。キリス
ト教では、この『旧約聖書』と『新約聖書』を
合わせて聖書と呼んでいます。

『旧約聖書』は作者不明で、神と人間との関係

ment and support to the hearts of many people around the world.

The difference between the two lies in their teachings. In contrast to Christ, who preached devotion to God as an absolute being, the Buddha denied the very notion that an absolute existed.

It also seems that there was a difference in how the two propagated their teachings. In contrast to Jesus who commanded that when the disciples went forth as missionaries they should go in groups of two or more, the Buddha told his disciples to go alone. It appears that during the time of the Buddha there was relative peace, whereas in Jesus' time Israel was under the control of Rome and there were many dangers.

The deaths of the two were also quite different. Christ was captured and crucified, but the Buddha lived to be eighty years old and was said to have been mourned at death by every living entity.

Q: What differences are there between the Bible and sutras?

The sutras are Buddhist scriptures which the disciples of the Buddha created by arranging and compiling the teachings of the Buddha.

In contrast, the Bible is made up of two parts, the Old Testament and the New Testament. The Old Testament is also the scripture of Judaism and it records historically the relationship between God and Israel from ancient times. The New Testament was compiled by the followers of Jesus Christ who revolutionized the thinking of Judaism, and it is composed of gospels and epistles. Christianity places the Old Testament and the New Testament together in one scripture called the Bible.

Because the Old Testament was written by unknown writ-

を描いた歴史書ですから、明らかにお経とは性格を異にします。しかし、『新約聖書』はキリストの死後、弟子たちがまとめた点、キリストの生涯や教えを説いている点などで、お経との共通性があります。

部派仏教の時代、涅槃（ねはん）を得るためには出家して修学・修行しなければならないという僧たちに反発し、だれでも仏になれるとして大乗仏教が生まれました。キリスト教もまた、救済されるためには厳しい戒律を遵守しなければならないとするユダヤ教に反発して生まれてきたものです。その意味では、キリスト教と『新約聖書』は、大乗仏教とその経典に比肩されるべきものなのかもしれません。

Q:「愛」という言葉の意味は、キリスト教と仏教ではどう違いますか？

180度違うといえます。キリスト教では「隣人を愛せ」といい、また「汝の敵を愛せ」と説きます。その時の愛は相手を慈（いつく）しむことであり、また相手の身になって考えてあげることでしょう。しかし、仏教ではこれを愛とはいわず、「慈悲（じひ）」と呼ぶのです。

仏教では、慈悲の「慈」は相手に楽を与えることで「与楽（よらく）」、「悲」は相手の苦しみを取ってあげることで「抜苦（ばっく）」といい、合わせて「与楽抜苦（よらくばっく）」などとも呼びます。これがキリスト教でいう愛の概念と近いものと思われます。

これに対して、仏教で「愛」という言葉で表されることは、「渇愛」ともいわれ、熱砂の中でのどの渇きに襲われ、水を欲しがるような激しい欲望を意味します。満足することを知らな

ers and because it is a historical piece portraying the relationship between God and humanity, it is clearly different in nature from sutras. However, the New Testament, in the sense that it was composed by disciples of Christ after his death and preaches the teachings of Christ while he was alive, bears some similarity with the sutras.

In the period of sectarian Buddhism, there was a revolt against the priests who held that in order to attain nirvana one had to become a priest and study and practice, and Mahayana Buddhism arose saying that anyone could become a buddha. Christianity too arose in reaction against Judaism which held that in order to gain salvation one had to obey strict precepts and customs. In this sense, Christianity and the New Testament may be analogous to Mahayana Buddhism and its scriptures.

Q: What is the difference between the word "love" in the Christian sense and in the Buddhist sense?

There is a hundred-eighty-degree difference. Christianity tells you to "love your neighbor" and "love your enemies." Love in that sense means having compassion for others and considering things from the other person's perspective. Buddhism, on the other hand, calls this not "love" but "compassion."

The two characters that make up the word *jihi*, compassion, refer to giving comfort to others and taking away their sufferings, and together this concept is expressed as "giving pleasure and removing suffering." This may be considered close to the concept of love within Christianity.

In contrast, that which is expressed in Buddhism as "love" is also called "thirst," in the sense of intense desire for water as one would have when assaulted by thirst in the middle of the desert. It is a desire that knows no satisfaction. Therefore,

い欲望です。だから、「愛」という言葉は、煩悩や貪欲と同じ意味で使われます。

　自分のものとして執着することともいいますから、男女間の愛は仏教でいう「愛」と共通しているのかもしれません。だから、愛は憎悪と背中合わせだといわれ、仏教では厭われるべきものとされているのです。

Q: 日本人は結婚式を神式でするのに、お葬式はなぜ仏式でするのですか？

　日本人の民族性として、汎神論いうものが染みついているからだと思われます。仏教が日本に伝えられる以前、日本人は八百万の神といって、木にも、岩にも、稲にも、山にも、川にも、海にも、あらゆるものに神が宿っていると信じていました。それらの神々が招き寄せられて宿る所が、神道でいうところの神社なのです。

　日本人が異国の宗教である仏教を受け入れることができたのも、この汎神論という体質があったからだと思います。つまり、日本人は日本の神々を、仏教で説く「仏」が仮の姿をとって現れたものと解釈し、神道と仏教の併存を可能にしてきたのです。

　日本人のそのような体質は、多くの宗教の中から一つを選び出して信仰するというよりも、どの宗教も排除せず、併せてご利益を願うという独特の信仰形態を形造ってきました。キリスト教とて例外ではありません。だから子供が生まれた時にはお宮参りをし、結婚式は神式やキリスト教の教会で挙げ、お葬式は仏式で行っても、日本人にはあまり抵抗感がないのでしょう。

"love" is used in the same sense as illusion and desire.

It also means attachment to someone as one's own, so the feelings that exist between man and woman are also called "love" in Buddhism, and in this sense the two meanings have something in common. Therefore, "love" is said to be the reverse side of "malice" and in Buddhism is considered something to abhor.

Q: Why is it that Japanese have Shintō weddings, and Buddhist funerals?

This results from the fact that as an ethnic group, the Japanese are imbued with pantheism. Prior to the transmission of Buddhism, Japanese believed in myriads of deities that inhabited all things: trees, rocks, rice plants, mountains, rivers, and the sea. According to Shintō, these gods are approached through shrines.

That the Japanese were able to embrace Buddhism, a religion from another country, was also due to this pantheistic tendency. That is, Japanese interpreted the deities of Japan to be transient manifestations of the *hotoke* preached by Buddhism, and the two have been allowed to co-exist.

Rather than select one religion out of a large number and believe in it, the Japanese predisposition has been to not exclude religions, but to incorporate them in a unique system of belief that seeks to benefit from them all. Not even Christianity is an exception. Therefore, the Japanese do not feel anything odd about paying a visit to a shrine when a child is born, holding a wedding in Shintō style or in a Christian church, and having a Buddhist funeral.

　しかし、これを見て日本人は宗教観念がない
と判断するのは誤りです。これこそ、日本民族
独特の宗教観念なのだと理解しなければ、日本
人の宗教観をとらえることは困難となるでしょ
う。

To judge from this that Japanese have no religious senti-
ment is a mistake. One must recognize that this itself is the religious sensibility of the Japanese as a ethnic group, or else it
will be very difficult to grasp how the Japanese people view
religion.

索　引
Index

日本語索引　　Japanese Index

【あ】
アーナンダ　34, 68, 186
アーリア人　20, 22
愛　58
阿育王山　116
愛別離苦　62
悪因悪果　66
阿修羅界（道）　48, 164
飛鳥時代　86
安土桃山時代　96
阿鼻地獄　168
尼　154
阿弥陀経　80
阿弥陀如来　44
阿弥陀仏　44
阿羅漢　32, 68

【い】
イエス・キリスト　24, 212
医王　54
伊邪那岐　204
伊邪那美　204
イスラム教　218
一乗止観院　106
一仏両祖　144
一向一揆　94, 136
一遍　92, 114, 140
位牌　176
因　64
印　130
因果　66
因果応報　66
インド・ヨーロッパ語族　20
因縁生起　64

【う】
有　60
ヴァイシャ　20
氏神　210
氏子　210
氏寺　86
ウパーリ　68
産土神　210
梅宮神社　210
盂蘭盆会　190

【え】
栄西　92, 116, 140
永平寺　142
回向　172
江戸時代　96
縁　64
延暦寺　90, 106

【お】
王侯　20
黄竜派　118
踊り念仏　140
お彼岸　190
お盆　190
折口信夫　198
怨憎会苦　62

【か】
カーシャパ　32
カースト　20
戒　128
階級制度　20
戒壇院西大寺　128
戒名　176
戒律　128

ガウタマ　20
餓鬼道　48
覚鑁　130
隠れキリシタン　96
過去七仏　42
柏手　202
春日神社　210
渇愛　216
合掌　202
カピラヴァスツ　20
カピラ城　20
神棚　208
伽藍　148
元興寺　126
元興寺縁起　82
鑑真　106, 126
ガンダーラ　28
神主　200
灌仏会　192
桓武天皇　90
観無量寿経　80
観無量寿経疏　108, 134

【き】
祇園精舎　34
飢餓界（道）　164
窺基　126
北枕　186
キャラバン　20
旧約聖書　214
経　198, 214
行　58
叫喚地獄　166
教行信証　110
教祖　206
経典　68
キリスト教　210

【く】
空海　90, 102, 128
クシナガラ　34, 186
クシャトリア　20
苦諦　54
百済　84
求不得苦　62

【け】
恵果　104

瑩山禅師　144
華厳経　80, 122
華厳宗　122
袈裟　160
解脱　48, 50, 148
結跏趺坐　186
結婚式　218
顕教　130
玄奘三蔵　126
顕如　136
建仁寺　142
憲法十七条　86

【こ】
虚庵懐敞　116, 140
公案　142
高句麗　84
興福寺　126
弘法大師　90, 104
高野山　90, 104
コーリヤ　24
五陰盛苦　62
五戒　156
黒縄地獄　166
国分寺　88
国分尼寺　88
極楽　44
極楽浄土　168
古事記　202, 204
五重の塔　148
五大　150
御仏前　178
御霊前　178
金剛界曼荼羅　82
金剛頂経　82
金剛峯寺　104, 128

【さ】
在家信者　128
最澄　90, 104
賽の河原　182
西遊記　126
坐禅　186
悟り　46, 50
沙羅双樹　34
三回忌　172
三教指帰　102
サンスクリット語　22

三途の川　182
三蔵　68
三衣一鉢　160
三宝　154

【し】
持戒　192
識　58
地獄界（道）　48, 164
司祭　20
時宗　92, 114, 140
四十九日　172
地蔵菩薩　44, 182
四諦　52
寺檀制度　96
シッダールタ　20
集諦　54
自灯明　38
慈悲　216
シャークヤ国　18
シャークヤ・ムニ　32
シャーラ樹　186
釈迦牟尼　32
取　58
受　58
十大弟子　34
シュードラ　20
十二因縁　52, 56
授戒　126, 178
綜芸種智院　104
手工業　20
衆合地獄　166
数珠　162, 188
出家　146, 154
シュッドーダナ　20
生　60, 62
荘園制　94
証空　134
上宮聖徳法王帝説　82
正見　54
正語　56
正業　56
上座部仏教　72
精舎　146
正思惟　54
正精進　56
正定　56
清浄光寺　140

小乗仏教　72
精進　192
精進料理　184
浄土　168
成道会　30
聖徳太子　86
浄土三部経　80
浄土宗　92, 96
浄土真宗　92, 134
焦熱地獄　168
正念　56
小品般若経　78
正命　56
成唯識論　126
浄瑠璃世界　44
昭和時代　98
諸行無常　60
触　58
庶民　20
除夜の鐘　188
新羅　84
自利　74
人界（道）　164
信空　134
真言宗　102
審祥　124
神道　196
真如　46
神仏分離令　98
新約聖書　214
親鸞　92, 110

【す，せ】
推古天皇　86
スーカラ・マッダヴァ　34
スジャーター　28
聖書　214
聖明王　84
青竜寺　104
絶対他力　136
善因善果　66
善光寺　114
専修念仏　108
禅定　192
善導　108
泉涌寺　128

【そ】
僧 152
僧伽 152
曹山本寂 144
葬式 218
総持寺 142
曹洞宗 94, 118, 142
蘇我氏 84
蘇我稲目 148
蘇我馬子 150
即身成仏 130
卒塔婆 148

【た】
他阿真教 140
大叫喚地獄 166
大正時代 98
大正デモクラシー 98
大焦熱地獄 168
大乗仏教 72, 156
胎蔵曼荼羅 82
大日経 82
大日如来 130
大般涅槃 48
大般涅槃経 36
大般若経 78
大品般若経 78
荼毘 170
タラーイ 18
陀羅尼 200
檀家 210

【ち】
智慧 192
知恩院 132
智 106, 132
畜生界（道）48, 164
智山派 130
智積院 130
地鎮祭 200
中陰 172
中有 172
中道 52
チュンダ 34
長谷寺 130

【て】
寺 148

天界（道）164
伝教大師 90, 106
天上天下唯我独尊 24
天台宗 92, 104
天道 48
転輪聖王 204

【と】
等活地獄 166
道元 92, 118, 142
洞山良价 144
唐招提寺 128
道昭 126, 170
道宣 128
道諦 54
東大寺 104

【な, に】
ナイランジャナー河 28
ナマス 76
南無 76
奈良時代 88
南都六宗 88, 122
尼僧 154
日蓮 92, 112
日蓮宗 92, 138
日本書紀 174, 202, 204
如浄 144
如来 44
人道 48
忍辱 192

【ね, の】
涅槃 46, 50
涅槃会 36
念珠 162
農業生産 20
祝詞 198

【は】
バーラーナシー 32
パーリ語 22
墓 170
八大寒地獄 166
八大熱地獄 166
八正道 52, 184
初宮詣 200
花祭り 192

バラモン　20
バラモン教　22
バラモンの儀式　22
般若経　78
般若心経　78
万物の創造主　212

【ひ】
比叡山　90, 106
ピッパラ樹　66
病　62
毘盧遮那仏　80, 122
ヒンドゥー教　22, 184

【ふ】
豊山派　130
布施　150, 192
仏教美術　206
仏像　206
仏壇　174, 208
仏土　168
仏塔　72
部派仏教　70
糞掃衣　160

【へ】
平家物語　36
平成時代　98
ペシャワール地方　28
弁長　134

【ほ】
法号　176, 178
法灯明　38
法然　92, 106
法名　176, 178
法華経　80, 112, 132, 138
菩薩　74
菩提　50
菩提寺　152
菩提樹　30, 66
法華一揆　94
法相宗　124
仏　44
本地垂迹説　208
梵天　30
梵網経　132

【ま】
マーヤー　20
マウリア王朝　70
摩訶止観　132
マガダ国　32
マハー・カーシャパ　68
マハー・プラジャーパティー　24
マヘーンドラ　72
曼荼羅　82
満中陰　172

【み】
水子地蔵　182
身延山久遠寺　138
名色　58
妙心寺派　142
妙法蓮華経　78, 80
弥勒仏　44
民族宗教　22

【む】
無我　60, 182
無間地獄　168
無常　60
無明　58
無量寿経　80
室町時代　94

【め, も】
明治時代　96
目覚めた者　42
滅諦　54
目連　190
本居宣長　198
物部氏　84

【や, ゆ, よ】
薬師寺　126
薬師如来　44
ヤショーダラー　26
唯識宗　124
遊行寺　114, 140
用命天皇　86
与楽抜苦　216

【り】
利他　74
利他救済　72

律 128
律宗 126
立正安国論 112, 138
臨済義玄 142
臨済宗 94, 116, 140
輪廻 48
輪廻転生 48, 166

【る, れ, ろ】
ルンビニー 22, 24

隷民 20
蓮如 94, 136
老 62
老死 60
良弁 124
六道 48, 164
六道輪廻 48, 166
六入 58
六波羅蜜 184
ロザリオ 162

英語索引　English Index

英語索引では日本の人名、地名、寺院名などの固有名詞、および日本語のローマ字読みは省きました。

【A】
absolute deity 219
absolute nirvana 49
absolute reliance 137
actions 59
agricultural production 21
all things are impermanent 61
alms 151
Amida Buddha 45
Amida Sutra 135
Amida Tathagata 45
Ananda 35, 69
animal 165
Arhat 33
arhat 69
Aryan 21, 23
Asoka 71
aspirant 43
Asuka period 87
asuras 165
attainment of buddhahood 31
Azuchi-Momoyama Period 95

【B】
bad cause bad effect 67
Baranasi 33
benefitting others 75
benefitting self 75

Bible 215
birth 61
bodhi 51
bodhi (bo) tree 31, 67
bodhisattva 75
bodhisattva Jizō 183
Brahman 21, 31
Brahmanism 23
Brahman rite 23
Buddha of Infinite Life Sutra, the 135
Buddha Vairocana 81
buddha-world 169
Buddhist altar 175
Buddhist art 207
Buddhist altar 209
Buddhist name 177
Buddhist surplice 161

【C】
caravan 21
caste 21, 65
Christianity 211
Chunda 35
clan temple 87
class society 21
clinging 59
commentary 69

commoners   21
compassion   217
condition   65
consciousness   59
Consciousness-Only sect   125
contact with external objects   59
creator of all things   213
cremation   171

【D】
decree separating Shinto and
    Buddhism   99
desiring pleasure and hatred   59
Diamond Realm Mandala   83, 131
Diamond-Peak Sutra, the   83
donations   151

【E】
Edo period   95
eight cold hells   167
eight hot hells   167
Eightfold Noble Path   53
emancipation   49, 51, 149
emancipation through benefitting
    others   73
enlightenment   47, 51
Esoteric Buddhism   103, 131
Essence of Prajna-paramita Sutra, the
    79
estate system   95
exclusive practice of the *nembutsu*
    109

【F】
family temple   153
first visit to a shrine of a newborn
    201
five great (elements)   151
five precepts   157
folk religion   23
founder   207
Four Noble Truths   53

【G】
Gandhara   29
Ganjin   127
Garland (Kegon) Sutra, the   81
Gautama   21

giving pleasure and removing
    suffering   217
good cause good effect   67
grave   171
Great Extinction, the   49
Great Sun Sutra, the   83
Greater-Vehicle Buddhism   77
ground-breaking ceremonies   201

【H】
handicrafts   21
heavenly beings   165
Heisei period   99
hell   165
hidden Christians   97
Hinayana Buddhism   73
Hinduism   23, 185
Hokke uprising   95
holy war   219
Hōnen   107
Hossō sect   125
humans   165
hungry spirits   165

【I】
ignorance   59
images of the Buddha   207
impermanence   61
*Indication of the Goals of the Three
    Teachings*   103
Islam   219

【J】
Jesus Christ   25, 213
Ji sect   93, 115, 141
Jizō Bosatsu   45
Jōdo sect   93, 107
Jōdo Shin sect   93, 135
Journey to the West, the   127

【K】
Kapila Palace   21
Kapilavastu   21, 23
karmic retribution   67
Kasyapa   33
Kegon Buddhism   123
Kegon Sutra, the   81
king of medicine   55

King Song 85
Koguryo 85
Kojiki, the 203, 205
Kshatriya 21
Kūkai 103
Kusinagara 35

【L】
lay believer 129
Lesser-Vehicle Buddhism 75
Lotus Sutra, the 79, 81, 113, 133, 139
lower class 21
Lumbini Garden 23, 25

【M】
Magadha 33
Mahakasyapa 69
Mahaprajapati 25
Mahavairocana Sutra, the 83
Mahayana Buddhism 73, 157
Mahendra 73
mandala 83, 131
Mandalas of the Two Realms 131
mantra 131
Mauria kingdom 73
Maya 23
Meditation on the Buddha of Infinite Life Sutra, the 135
Meiji period 97
memorial tablet 177
Middle Path 53
Miroku Buddha 45
mudra 131
Muromachi period 95

【N】
Nairanjana River 29
Nara period 89
nembutsu dance 141
New Testament, the 215
Nichiren 113
Nichiren sect 93, 139
Nihon Shoki, the 173, 203, 205
nirvana 47, 51
non-self 183
nothing has an ego 61

【O】
objects of consciousness 59
old age and death 61
Old Testament, the 215
One Buddha and the Two Founders 145

【P, Q】
Paekche 85
pagoda 149
Pali 23
paradise 45
past seven buddhas 43
Peshawar region 29
pippala 67
posthumous name 177
power of the other 137
precept 69, 129
priest 21, 153
Prince Shōtoku 87
Pure Land 169
Pure Lapis-Lazuli World 45
Queen Maya 21

【R】
receiving the precepts 127, 179
Records of Gangōji 83
regulation 129
reincarnation 49
reincarnation within the six realms 49
right action 57
right endeavor 57
right living 57
right meditation 57
right memory 57
right speech 57
right thinking 55
right view 55
Rinzai sect 95, 117, 141
Ritsu sect 127
River of Three Crossings 183
rosary 163
royalty 21

【S】
Sakya Tribe 19
Sakya-muni 33

sala tree   187
Sanskrit   23
seated meditation   187
sectarian Buddhism   71
sensation   59
Seventeen-Article Constitution, the   87
Shingon Buddhism   103
Shingon sect   131
Shintō altar   209
Shintō priests   201
Shintoism   197
Shōwa period   99
Siddhartha   21
Silla   85
six entrances   59
six paths   49, 165
six sects of Nara Buddhism   123
Six Southern Sects   89
Sōtō school of Zen   119
Sōtō sect   95, 143
state of existence in transmigration   61
string of beads   163
stupa   73, 149
Suddhodana   21
Sudra   21
Sujata   29
Sukara-maddava   35
sutra   69, 199, 215
Sutra of the Garland Buddhas   123
Sutra of the Great Extinction, the   37
Sutra of the Lotus of the Wonderful Law, the   79

【T】
Taishō Democracy   99
Taishō period   99
Tale of the Heike, the   37
Tarai   19
Tathagata   45
Teaching, Practice, Faith, Attainment   111
temple   149
Ten Great Disciples   35
Tendai Lotus sect   133
Tendai sect   93, 105, 131
Theravada   73

thirst   217
Three Baskets   69
Three Stores   69
thusness   47
Traditions concerning His Holiness, Prince Shōtoku   83
transfer of merit   173
transmigration   49
transmigration of the soul   167
transmigration within the six realms   167
Treatise on the Establishment of the Doctrine of Consciousness Only   127
Treatise on the Establishment of the True Dharma and the Peace of the Nation   113, 139
Triple Pure Land Sutras, the   81, 135
Truth of Cause   55
Truth of Extinction   55
Truth of Suffering   55
Truth of the Path   55
Twelve Causes   53, 57

【U，V】
Upali   69
Vairocana   123
Vaisya   21
Virgin Mary   25

【W】
way of animals   49
way of asuras   49
way of beings in hell   49
way of devas   49
way of human beings   49
way of *pretas*   49
weddings   201
Wisdom (Prahna) Sutra   79
Womb Realm Mandala   131

【Y】
Yasodhara   27

英語で話す「仏教」Q&A
Talking About Buddhism　Q&A

1997年11月10日　第1刷発行
1999年2月25日　第2刷発行

著　者　高田佳人

翻訳者　ジェームス・M・バーダマン

発行者　野間佐和子

発行所　講談社インターナショナル株式会社
　　　　〒112-8652　東京都文京区音羽1-17-14
　　　　電話：03-3944-6493（編集）
　　　　　　　03-3944-6492（営業）

印刷所　大日本印刷株式会社

製本所　株式会社　堅省堂

落丁本、乱丁本は、講談社インターナショナル営業部宛にお送りください。送料小社負担にてお取替えいたします。なお、この本についてのお問い合わせは、編集局第二出版部宛にお願いいたします。本書の無断複写（コピー）は著作権法上での例外を除き、禁じられています。

定価はカバーに表示してあります。

Copyright © 1997 by Takada Yoshihito and James M. Vardaman, Jr.
ISBN4-7700-2161-5

講談社バイリンガル・ブックス

英語で読んでも面白い！

- 楽しく読めて自然に英語が身に付くバイリンガル表記
- 実用から娯楽まで読者の興味に応える多彩なテーマ
- 重要単語、表現法がひと目で分かる段落対応レイアウト

46判変型（113 x 188 mm）仮製

英語で話す「日本」Q&A
Talking About Japan Q & A

KBB 1

講談社インターナショナル 編　　　　320ページ　ISBN 4-7700-2026-0

外国の人と話すとき、必ず出てくる話題は「日本」のこと。でも英語力よりも前に困るのは、日本について知らないことがいっぱいという事実です。政治、経済から文化までモヤモヤの知識をスッキリさせてくれる「日本再発見」の書。

イラスト 日本まるごと事典
Japan at a Glance

KBB 17

インターナショナル・インターンシップ・プログラムス 著　　256ページ（2色刷）　ISBN 4-7700-2080-5

1000点以上のイラストを使って日本のすべてを紹介──自然、文化、社会はもちろんのこと、折り紙の折り方、着物の着方から、ナベで米を炊く方法や「あっちむいてホイ」の遊び方まで国際交流に必要な知識とノウハウを満載。

英語で折り紙
Origami in English

KBB 3

山口 真 著　　　　168ページ　ISBN 4-7700-2027-9

たった一枚の紙から無数の造形が生まれ出る‥‥外国の人たちは、その面白さに目を見張ります。折るとき、英語で説明できるようにバイリンガルにしました。ホームステイ、留学、海外駐在に必携の一冊です。

英語で日本料理
100 Recipes from Japanese Cooking

辻調理師専門学校　畑耕一郎, 近藤一樹 著
272ページ（カラー口絵16ページ）　ISBN 4-7700-2079-1

外国の人と親しくなる最高の手段は、日本料理を作ってあげること、そしてその作り方を教えてあげることです。代表的な日本料理100品の作り方を、外国の計量法も入れながら、バイリンガルで分かりやすく説明します。

英語で話す国際経済 Q&A　一目で分かるキーワード図解付き
A Bilingual Guide to the World Economy

KBB 37

日興リサーチセンター 著　マーク・ショルツ 訳　320ページ　ISBN 4-7700-2164-X

不安定な要素をかかえて流動する国際経済の複雑なメカニズムを、日本最良のシンクタンクのひとつ、日興リサーチセンターが、最新の情報をおりこみながら初心者にも分かるようにやさしく解説。

英語で話す日本ビジネス Q&A　ここが知りたい、日本のカイシャ
Frequently Asked Questions on Corporate Japan

KBB 36

米山司理、リチャード・ネイサン 著　320ページ　ISBN 4-7700-2165-8

「世界市場で高いシェアを誇る日本の会社は？」「日本で最も古い会社」「日本の企業の世界での実力」「世界に通用する名経営者は誰？」「郵便局は世界最大の銀行？」など、日本の会社の人と組織について日本人も詳しく知りたい情報満載！

英語で読む日本史
Japanese History : 11 Experts Reflect on the Past

KBB 4

英文日本大事典 編　232ページ　ISBN 4-7700-2024-4

11人の超一流ジャパノロジストたちが英語で書き下ろした日本全史。外国人の目から見た日本史はどういうものか、また日本の歴史事項を英語で何と表現するのか。新しい視点が想像力をかき立てます。

日本を創った100人
100 Japanese You Should Know

KBB 25

板坂 元 監修　英文日本大事典 編　240ページ　ISBN 4-7700-2159-3

混沌と激動を乗り越え築き上げられた現在の日本。その長い歴史の節目節目で大きな役割を果たした歴史上のキーパーソン100人を、超一流のジャパノロジストたちが解説。グローバルな大競争時代を迎えた今、彼らの生き方が大きな指針となります。

英語で話す「日本の謎」Q&A　外国人が聞きたがる100のWHY
100 Tough Questions for Japan

KBB 11

板坂 元 監修　248ページ　ISBN 4-7700-2091-0

なぜ、結婚式は教会で、葬式はお寺でなんてことができるの？　なぜ、大人までがマンガを読むの？　なぜ、時間とお金をかけてお茶を飲む練習をするの？——こんな外国人の問いをつきつめてゆくと、日本文化の核心が見えてきます。

英語で話す「雑学ニッポン」Q&A
Japan Trivia

KBB 35

素朴な疑問探究会 編 　　　　　　　　　272ページ　ISBN 4-7700-2361-8

日本にいる外国人と飲んでいて、一番盛りあがる話はなんといっても、「ニッポンの謎」についての雑学です。「日本の女性は、なぜ下唇から口紅を塗るの？」「なぜ"鈴木"という名字が多いの？」など、外国人が疑問に思う「なぜ？」に答えます。

英語で話す「日本の心」　和英辞典では引けないキーワード197
Keys to the Japanese Heart and Soul

KBB 12

英文日本大事典 編 　　　　　　　　　328ページ　ISBN 4-7700-2082-1

一流のジャパノロジスト53人が解説した「日本の心」を知るためのキーワード集。「わび」「さび」「義理人情」「甘え」「根回し」「談合」「みそぎ」など、日本人特有な「心の動き」を外国人に説明するための強力なツールです。

英語で話す「日本の文化」
Japan as I See It

KBB 22

NHK国際放送局文化プロジェクト 編　ダン・ケニー 訳　208ページ　ISBN 4-7700-2197-6

金田一春彦、遠藤周作、梅原猛、平川祐弘、西堀栄三郎、鯖田豊之、野村万作、井上靖、小松左京、中根千枝の10人が、日本文化の「謎」を解く。NHKの国際放送で21の言語で放送され、分かりやすいと世界中で大好評。

もう一つの母国、日本へ
Living in Two Countries

KBB 38

ドナルド・キーン 著　塩谷 紘 訳　　　224ページ　ISBN 4-7700-2455-X

著者が生まれた国、アメリカと自分の精神を育ててくれた国、日本という2つの祖国の狭間に生きる著名なジャパノロジストが、日本への熱い思いを込めて語る、日本社会の独特の仕組みや日本人の風習についての痛烈な意見。

ニッポン不思議発見！　日本文化を英語で語る50の名エッセイ集
Discover Japan: Words, Customs and Concepts

KBB 14

日本文化研究所 編　松本道弘 訳　　　272ページ　ISBN 4-7700-2142-9

絶望的な場合ですら、日本人は「そこをなんとか」という言葉を使って、相手に甘えようとする……こんな指摘をうけると、いかに日本人は独特なものの考え方をしているか分かります。あなたも「不思議」を発見してみませんか。

ニッポン見聞録　大好きな日本人に贈る新・開国論
Heisei Highs and Lows

KBB 8

トム・リード 著　　　　　　　　　　224ページ　ISBN 4-7700-2092-9

国際化の進む日本ですが、アメリカのジャーナリストが鋭い目と耳で浮き彫りにしたニッポンの姿は、驚くほど平穏でといおしく、恥ずかしいくらい強欲で無知なものでした。トムが大好きな日本人へ贈る新・開国論。

「Japan」クリッピング ワシントン・ポストが書いた「日本」
Views of Japan from The Washington Post Newsroom

KBB 6

東郷茂彦 著　　　　　264ページ　ISBN 4-7700-2023-6

アメリカの世論をリードするワシントン・ポストに書かれた「Japan」……政治、外交、経済、社会のジャンルで取り上げられた日本の姿を、国際ジャーナリストが解説し、その背後にある問題点を浮き彫りにする一冊。

開国ノススメ 孤立化するニッポンへの問題提起
Open up, Japan!

KBB 31

アンドリュー・ホルバート 著　　　　　208ページ　ISBN 4-7700-2348-0

欧米の高級紙誌で活躍する一流の国際ジャーナリストが、海外で問われることの多い、日本の政治・経済・社会システムの問題について「どのように説明すればよいか」のヒントを与えてくれます。

「縮み」志向の日本人
Smaller is Better

KBB 33

李 御寧 著　　　　　200ページ　ISBN 4-7700-2445-2

一寸法師から、盆栽、箱庭、茶室、俳句にいたるまで、常に小さいものを求め、小さいものへ向かう「縮み志向」。言語・風俗・文化などが似ており、また日本文化にも影響を与えた韓国、その初代文化大臣を務めた著者によって発見された日本文化の本質。

NHK「ニュースのキーワード」
NHK: Key Words in the News

KBB 26

NHK国際放送局 「ニュースのキーワード」プロジェクト 編　　　　　232ページ　ISBN 4-7700-2342-1

日本で話題になっている時事問題を解説する、NHK国際放送の番組「ニュースのキーワード」から「総会屋」「日本版ビッグバン」「ダイオキシン」など、33のキーワードを収録しました。国際的観点からの解説が、現代の日本の姿を浮き彫りにします。

NHK「日本ひとくち歳時記」
Around the Year in Japan

KBB 32

NHK国際放送局 「日本一口事典」プロジェクト 編　　　　　256ページ　ISBN 4-7700-2457-6

ひな祭り、七夕、運動会、年賀状など季節感あふれる32のキーワードから、日本文化を斬新な視点で、簡潔に分かりやすく解説します。21ヵ国語で放送中のNHK国際放送局が発見した「ニッポン」。

ベスト・オブ・天声人語
VOX POPULI, VOX DEI

KBB 23

朝日新聞論説委員室 著　　朝日イブニングニュース 訳　　　　　288ページ　ISBN 4-7700-2166-6

「天声人語」は「朝日新聞」の名コラムというよりも、日本を代表するコラムです。香港返還、アムラー現象、たまごっち、マザー・テレサの死など、現代を読み解く傑作56編を、社会・世相、政治、スポーツなどのジャンル別に収録しました。

誤解される日本人　外国人がとまどう41の疑問
The Inscrutable Japanese

KBB 20

メリディアン・リソーシス・アソシエイツ 編　賀川 洋 著　　232ページ　ISBN 4-7700-2129-1

あなたのちょっとした仕草や表情が大きな誤解を招いているかもしれません。「日本人はどんなときに誤解を受けるのか？」そのメカニズムを解説し、「どのように外国人に説明すればよいか」最善の解決策を披露します。

英語で話す「アメリカ」Q&A
Talking About the USA Q & A

KBB 21

賀川 洋 著　　312ページ　ISBN 4-7700-2005-8

仕事でも留学でも遊びでも、アメリカ人と交際するとき、知っておくと役に立つ「アメリカ小事典」。アメリカ人の精神と社会システムにポイントをおいた解説により、自然、歴史、政治、文化、そして人をバイリンガルで紹介します。

英語で話す「世界」Q&A
Talking About the World Q & A

KBB 19

講談社インターナショナル 編　　320ページ　ISBN 4-7700-2006-6

今、世界にはいくつの国家があるか、ご存じですか？　対立をはらみながらも、急速に1つの運命共同体になっていく「世界」──外国の人と話すとき知らなければならない「世界」に関する国際人必携の「常識集」です。

イラスト 日米ジェスチャー事典
The Illustrated Handbook of American and Japanese Gestures

KBB 34

スティーブン・N・ウイリアムス 著　　264ページ　ISBN 4-7700-2344-8

知らなかったではすまされない──。誤解を受け、国際問題や大騒動を引き起こしかねない、日本とアメリカのジェスチャーの違いを、ひと目で分かるイラストで解説します。言葉よりモノをいう780のジェスチャー。

ドタンバのマナー
The Ultimate Guide to Etiquette in Japan

KBB 27

サトウサンペイ 著　　240ページ（オールカラー）　ISBN 4-7700-2193-3

サンペイ流家元が自らしでかした「日常のヘマ」「海外でのヘマ」を一目で分かるようにマンガにした、フレッシュマンに贈る究極のマナー集。新社会人必読！知っていればすむことなのに、知らないために嫌われたり、憎まれてはかないません。

アメリカ日常生活のマナーQ&A
Do As Americans Do

KBB 13

ジェームス・M・バーダマン、倫子・バーダマン 著　　264ページ　ISBN 4-7700-2128-3

"How do you do?" に "How do you do?" と答えてはいけないということ、ご存知でしたか？　日本では当たり前と思われていたことがマナー違反だったのです。旅行で、駐在で、留学でアメリカに行く人必携のマナー集。

日米比較 冠婚葬祭のマナー
Do It Right : Japanese & American Social Etiquette

ジェームス・M・バーダマン，倫子・バーダマン 著　　　　192ページ　ISBN 4-7700-2025-2

アメリカでは結婚式や葬式はどのように行われるのか？　お祝いや香典は？……そしてアメリカの人たちも、日本の事情を知りたがります。これだけあればもう困らない。日米冠婚葬祭マニュアル、バイリンガル版。

茶の本
The Book of Tea

岡倉天心 著　千 宗室 序と跋　浅野 晃 訳　　　　264ページ　ISBN 4-7700-2379-0

一碗の茶をすする、そのささやかで簡潔な行為の中に、偉大な精神が宿っている──茶道によせて、日本と東洋の精神文化の素晴らしさを明かし、アジアの理想が回復されることを英文で呼びかけた本書は、日本の心を英語で明かす不朽の名著。

武士道
BUSHIDO

新渡戸稲造 著　須知徳平 訳　　　　312ページ　ISBN 4-7700-2402-9

「日本が生んだ最大の国際人」新渡戸博士が英語で著した世界的名著。「日本の精神文化を知る最良の書」として世界17ヵ国語に翻訳され、1世紀にわたって読みつがれてきた不滅の日本人論。国際人必読の1冊。

英語で話す「仏教」Q&A
Talking About Buddhism Q & A

高田佳人 著　ジェームス・M・バーダマン 訳　　　　240ページ　ISBN 4-7700-2161-5

四十九日までに7回も法事をするのは、「亡くなった人が7回受ける裁判をこの世から応援するため」だということ、ご存じでしたか？　これだけは知っておきたい「仏教」に関することがらを、やさしい英語で説明できるようにした入門書です。

ビジュアル 英語で読む日本国憲法
The Constitution of Japan

英文日本大百科事典 編　　　　208ページ　ISBN 4-7700-2191-7

難しいと思っていた「日本国憲法」も、英語で読むと不思議とよく分かります。日本国憲法を、59点の写真を使って、バイリンガルで分かりやすく解説しました。条文中に出てくる難解な日本語には、ルビや説明がついています。

まんが 日本昔ばなし
Once Upon a Time in Japan

川内彩友美 編　ラルフ・マッカーシー 訳　　　　160ページ　ISBN 4-7700-2173-9

人気テレビシリーズ「まんが日本昔ばなし」から、「桃太郎」「金太郎」「一寸法師」など、より抜きの名作8話をラルフ・マッカーシーの名訳でお届けします。ホームステイなどでも役に立つ一冊です。

まんが 日本昔ばなし 妖しのお話
Once Upon a Time in *Ghostly* Japan

KBB 29

川内彩友美 編　ラルフ・マッカーシー 訳　　　　　152ページ　ISBN 4-7700-2347-2

妖しく、怖く、心に響く昔ばなしの名作を英語で読む。人気テレビシリーズ「まんが日本昔ばなし」から、「鶴の恩返し」「雪女」「舌切り雀」「耳なし芳一」「分福茶釜」など8話を収録しました。

ベスト・オブ 宮沢賢治短編集
The Tales of Miyazawa Kenji

KBB 5

宮沢賢治 著　ジョン・ベスター 訳　　　　　216ページ　ISBN 4-7700-2081-3

「注文の多い料理店」「どんぐりと山猫」「祭の晩」「鹿踊りのはじまり」「土神ときつね」「オツベルと象」「毒もみの好きな署長さん」「セロ弾きのゴーシュ」の代表作8編を精選。ジョン・ベスターの名訳でどうぞ。

銀河鉄道の夜
Night Train to the Stars

KBB 10

宮沢賢治 著　ジョン・ベスター 訳　　　　　184ページ　ISBN 4-7700-2131-3

賢治童話の中でも最も人気の高い「銀河鉄道の夜」は、賢治の宗教心と科学精神が反映された独特の世界——天空、自然、大地がみごとに描かれ、光と音と動きに満ち溢れています。ジョバンニと一緒に銀河を旅してみませんか。

ベスト・オブ 窓ぎわのトットちゃん
Best of Totto-chan : The Little Girl at the Window

KBB 9

黒柳徹子 著　ドロシー・ブリトン 訳　　　　　240ページ　ISBN 4-7700-2127-5

小学校一年生にして「退学」になったトットちゃんは、転校先の校長先生に「君は本当はいい子なんだよ」と温かい言葉のシャワーで励まされます…バイリンガル版で、あの空前の大ベストセラーの感動をもう一度！

マザー・グース　愛される唄70選
Mother Goose : 70 Nursery Rhymes

KBB 7

谷川俊太郎 訳　渡辺 茂 解説　　　　　184ページ　ISBN 4-7700-2078-3

「マイ・フェア・レディー」や「お熱いのがお好き」という題名も、マザー・グースからの引用だったってこと、ご存じでしたか？　英米人にとって必須教養であるこの童謡集を、詩人・谷川俊太郎の名訳と共にお楽しみください。

講談社バイリンガル・ブックス　（オン・カセット）　英語で聞いても面白い！

印のタイトルは、英文テキスト部分を録音したカセット・テープが発売されています。本との併用により聞く力・話す力を高め、実用的な英語が身につく格好のリスニング教材です。

ビジネスマン必携！

対訳 英語で話す日本経済Q&A
A Bilingual Guide to the Japanese Economy

NHK国際放送局経済プロジェクト・
大和総研経済調査部 編

46判 (128 x 188 mm) 仮製 368ページ

ISBN 4-7700-1942-4

NHK国際放送で好評を得た番組が本になりました。クイズと
会話形式で楽しく読んでいくうちに、日本経済の仕組が分かり、
同時に英語にも強くなっていきます。日本語と英語の対応が
ひと目で分かる編集上の工夫もいっぱい。

名作＋名訳＋名画の魅力！

対訳 おくのほそ道
The Narrow Road to Oku

松尾芭蕉 著 ドナルド・キーン 訳
宮田雅之 切り絵

A5判変型 (140 x 226 mm)
仮製 188ページ（カラー口絵41点）
ISBN 4-7700-2028-7

古典文学の最高峰のひとつ「おくのほそ道」を、ドナルド・
キーンが新訳しました。画家、宮田雅之が精魂を込めた切り絵
の魅力とあいまって、この名作に新しい生命が吹き込まれた、
必読の1冊です。

対訳 竹取物語
The Tale of the Bamboo Cutter

川端康成 現代語訳
ドナルド・キーン 英訳
宮田雅之 切り絵

A5判変型 横長 (226 x 148 mm)
仮製 箱入り180ページ（カラー口絵16点）
ISBN 4-7700-2329-4

ノーベル賞作家の現代語訳と傑出した芸術家の作品、そして
日本文学の研究に一生を捧げたジャパノロジストの翻訳が合
体した、大人のための「竹取物語」。

わが家の味を海外に

バイリンガル とってもかんたんマイレシピ
Stone Soup : Easy Japanese Home Cooking

渡辺節子 著

B5判変型 (189 x 257 mm) 仮製 256ページ

ISBN 4-7700-2061-9

手軽な日本の家庭料理、わが家の味160品目の作り方を英語
と日本語で紹介したクッキングブック。作り方や調理器具な
どのイラスト付き、カロリー計算・調理時間もひと目で分か
ります。

対訳 日本事典 （全1巻）
The Kodansha Bilingual Encyclopedia of Japan

講談社インターナショナル 編

B5判 (182 x 257 mm)
上製　箱入り
944ページ（カラー口絵16ページ）
ISBN 4-7700-2130-5

ビジネス、海外駐在、
留学、ホームステイなど、
さまざまな国際交流の場で、
幅広くご活用いただけます。

特色

「日本」を国際的な視点で理解できる幅広い知識と、
実用的な英語が身につきます。

1. 現代の政治制度、最新の経済情報を豊富に記載し、日本を総合的に理解できる。
2. 分野別の構成により、テーマに沿って自然に読み進むことができる。
3. 豊富なイラストと図版を収録し、完全対訳のレイアウトと欄外のキーワードで、重要単語や表現の日英相互参照に便利。
4. 日本国憲法、重要な国際条約、年表をいずれも日英併記で巻末に収録。
5. 英語からも日本語（ローマ字）からも引けるインデックスつき。

内容構成

地理 / 歴史 / 政治 / 経済 / 社会 / 文化 / 生活